Microsoft SharePoint 2010 Business Application Blueprints

Master SharePoint application development by building exciting SharePoint business solutions

Mike Oryszak

BIRMINGHAM - MUMBAI

Microsoft SharePoint 2010 Business Application Blueprints

First published: June 2012

Production Reference: 1180612

Published by Packt Publishing Ltd.
Livery Place
35 Livery Street
Birmingham B3 2PB, UK.

ISBN 978-1-84968-360-9

www.packtpub.com

Cover Image by Artie Ng (artherng@yahoo.com.au)

Credits

Author
Mike Oryszak

Reviewers
Michael Nemtsev

Doug Ortiz

Wei Chung, Low

Acquisition Editor
Rashmi Phadnis

Lead Technical Editor
Shreerang Deshpande

Technical Editors
Manmeet Singh Vasir

Felix Vijay

Rati Pillai

Project Coordinator
Vishal Bodwani

Proofreader
Bernadette Watkins

Indexer
Monica Ajmera Mehta

Graphics
Manu Joseph

Production Coordinator
Nilesh R. Mohite

Cover Work
Nilesh R. Mohite

About the Author

Mike Oryszak is a Consultant and Practice Manager with **Intellinet**, a Microsoft Gold-Certified partner located in the South Eastern US. Mike works with customers to design and implement business solutions that leverage SharePoint as a platform. Mike is actively involved in the SharePoint community as the leader of the **Triangle SharePoint User Group** in Raleigh, NC, as well as a frequent speaker at SharePoint events and conferences. Mike has been recognized for his community involvement as a three time Microsoft Valuable Professional (MVP) for SharePoint Server. When not working, Mike can be found at home with his family or off hiking the many trails in the mountains of western North Carolina. Mike can be reached at `nextconnect@live.com` or through his blog at `http://www.mikeoryszak.com`.

A project like this is a very big undertaking, one that cannot be completed without a supporting team. I would like to thank my colleagues at Intellinet for their encouragement as well as my many friends in the SharePoint community who have helped me challenge ideas and evolve my understanding of best practices over time. I would also like to give a special thank you to the team at Packt Publishing for their guidance in helping me mold these thoughts into a cohesive package.

The time commitment for a project like this is pretty big and a lot of personal sacrifices had to be made. I would like to thank my family for sticking with me through this arduous journey and for providing their never-ending support.

About the Reviewers

Michael Nemtsev is an ex-Microsoft MVP in .NET/C# and SharePoint Server 2010 (2005 to 2011).

Michael's expertise is in Enterprise Integration and Platform & Collaborations areas and he is currently working as a Senior Consultant at Microsoft in Sydney, Australia, helping clients to improve business collaboration with SharePoint 2010 and Office365.

Doug Ortiz is an Independent Consultant whose skill set encompasses multiple platforms such as .NET, SharePoint, Office, and SQL Server.

He possesses a Master's Degree in Relational Databases and has over 20 years of experience in Information Technology, of which half are in .NET and SharePoint. His roles have ranged from architecture, implementation, administration, disaster recovery, migrations, development and automation of information systems, both in and outside of SharePoint.

He is the founder of Illustris, LLC and can be reached at: dougortiz@illustris.org.

Interesting aspects of his profession include:

- He has experience integrating multiple platforms and products with the purpose of sharing data
- He has improved, salvaged, and architected projects by utilizing unique and innovative techniques

When not working, his hobbies include yoga and scuba diving.

I would like to thank my wonderful wife Mila for all her help and support, as well as Maria and Nikolay.

I would also like to thank everyone at Packt Publishing for their encouragement and guidance.

Wei Chung, a Technical Lead in BizTalk and .NET and an MCT, MCPD, MCITP, MCTS, MCSD.NET, works with ResMed (NYSE: RMD), at its Kuala Lumpur, Malaysia, campus. He is also a member of PMI, certified as a PMP. He started working on Microsoft .NET since its early career and has been involved in development, consultation, and corporate training in the area of business intelligence, system integration, and virtualization. He has also worked for the Bursa Malaysia (formerly Kuala Lumpur Stock Exchange) and previously for Shell IT International, which provided him with rich integration experience across different platforms.

He strongly believes that a great system implementation delivers precious value to the business, and integration of various systems across different platforms will always be a part of this; just as people from different and diverse cultures live together in most of the major cities, in harmony.

www.PacktPub.com

Support files, eBooks, discount offers and more

You might want to visit www.PacktPub.com for support files and downloads related to your book.

Did you know that Packt offers eBook versions of every book published, with PDF and ePub files available? You can upgrade to the eBook version at www.PacktPub.com and as a print book customer, you are entitled to a discount on the eBook copy. Get in touch with us at service@packtpub.com for more details.

At www.PacktPub.com, you can also read a collection of free technical articles, sign up for a range of free newsletters and receive exclusive discounts and offers on Packt books and eBooks.

http://PacktLib.PacktPub.com

Do you need instant solutions to your IT questions? PacktLib is Packt's online digital book library. Here, you can access, read and search across Packt's entire library of books.

Why Subscribe?

- Fully searchable across every book published by Packt
- Copy and paste, print and bookmark content
- On demand and accessible via web browser

Free Access for Packt account holders

If you have an account with Packt at www.PacktPub.com, you can use this to access PacktLib today and view nine entirely free books. Simply use your login credentials for immediate access.

Instant Updates on New Packt Books

Get notified! Find out when new books are published by following @PacktEnterprise on Twitter, or the *Packt Enterprise* Facebook page.

Table of Contents

Preface

This book will dive into a diverse set of real-world scenarios to deliver sample business solutions that can serve as the foundation for your own solutions. It draws from the author's extensive experience with SharePoint to leverage the platform's underlying services to provide solutions that can support social collaboration, content and document management, as well as project collaboration. Each chapter represents a new business solution that builds on the overall platform to deliver more complex solutions and more advanced techniques. By the end of the book, the reader will understand how to leverage the SharePoint platform to build their own business solutions.

What this book covers

Chapter 1, Building an Effective Intranet: An Effective Intranet Site for your organization that maximizes the site's ability to aggregate content and is highly effective at communicating important messages.

Chapter 2, Building an Out of Office Delegation Solution: A Workflow Out of Office Solution that allows users to manage their out of office dates and automate task assignments to a delegated resource.

Chapter 3, Building an Enterprise Content Management Solution: An Enterprise Content Management solution designed to support large scale document repositories with the ability to route documents automatically between site collections based on metadata attributes along with custom solutions for surfacing the relevant content.

Chapter 4, Building an Engaging Community Site: An Engaging Community Site including custom features that can be used to enhance collaboration and provide an information sharing system.

Chapter 5, Building a Site Request and Provisioning System: A Site Request and Provisioning System that supports automated site provisioning for user requested sites in a way that supports complex dynamic feature activation and configuration.

Chapter 6, Building a Project Site Template: An overview of the template methods available with SharePoint along with a detailed approach for creating web templates in order to create a project site template to support project initiatives and track Issues, Tasks, and Contacts.

Chapter 7, Building a Project Management Main Site: A Project Management Main Site demonstrating a solution that can aggregate the key metrics and status information from the project management sites created in the previous chapter.

Chapter 8, Building a Task Rollup Solution: Create custom Web Parts that can aggregate tasks from the specified sites.

Chapter 9, Building a Site Directory with SharePoint Search: Solutions to leverage SharePoint Search to provide an optimized experience making it easier for users to search and discover relevant sites.

Bonus Chapter, Understanding SharePoint Development Choices: This chapter provides a brief overview of the different customization options that are available, tools that can be used to create them, as well as some additional considerations when choosing a development path.

You can download the Bonus Chapter from: `http://www.packtpub.com/sites/default/files/downloads/SharePoint_development.pdf`

What you need for this book

This chapter will require the following software:

- SharePoint Server 2010 Enterprise
- Visual Studio 2010 Professional
- SharePoint Designer 2010

Who this book is for

This book is for SharePoint developers, consultants, and administrators who want to build a range of SharePoint solutions that extend the SharePoint platform, and see how to apply the many available SharePoint features in different scenarios.

Conventions

In this book, you will find a number of styles of text that distinguish between different kinds of information. Here are some examples of these styles, and an explanation of their meaning.

Code words in text are shown as follows:
"The `ExecuteOrDelayUntilScriptLoaded()` function will delay the execution of the script until the page and all scripts are loaded."

A block of code is set as follows:

```
var statusId = '';
var isitDlg = window.location.href.match(/isDlg/i) != null;

if (!isitDlg) {
    ExecuteOrDelayUntilScriptLoaded(LoadNotifications, "sp.js");
}
```

When we wish to draw your attention to a particular part of a code block, the relevant lines or items are set in bold:

```
<WebPartPages:WebPartZone runat="server"
AllowPersonalization="false" ID="TopZone" FrameType="TitleBarOnly"
Title="<%$Resources:cms,WebPartZoneTitle_Top%>"
Orientation="Horizontal">
```

New terms and **important words** are shown in bold. Words that you see on the screen, in menus or dialog boxes for example, appear in the text like this: "After creating the library, create a page and select the **Page** tab".

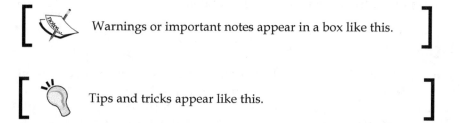

> Warnings or important notes appear in a box like this.

> Tips and tricks appear like this.

Reader feedback

Feedback from our readers is always welcome. Let us know what you think about this book—what you liked or may have disliked. Reader feedback is important for us to develop titles that you really get the most out of.

To send us general feedback, simply send an e-mail to feedback@packtpub.com, and mention the book title through the subject of your message.

If there is a topic that you have expertise in and you are interested in either writing or contributing to a book, see our author guide on www.packtpub.com/authors.

Customer support

Now that you are the proud owner of a Packt book, we have a number of things to help you to get the most from your purchase.

Downloading the example code

You can download the example code files for all Packt books you have purchased from your account at http://www.packtpub.com. If you purchased this book elsewhere, you can visit http://www.packtpub.com/support and register to have the files e-mailed directly to you.

Errata

Although we have taken every care to ensure the accuracy of our content, mistakes do happen. If you find a mistake in one of our books—maybe a mistake in the text or the code—we would be grateful if you would report this to us. By doing so, you can save other readers from frustration and help us improve subsequent versions of this book. If you find any errata, please report them by visiting http://www.packtpub.com/support, selecting your book, clicking on the **errata submission form** link, and entering the details of your errata. Once your errata are verified, your submission will be accepted and the errata will be uploaded to our website, or added to any list of existing errata, under the Errata section of that title.

Piracy

Piracy of copyright material on the Internet is an ongoing problem across all media. At Packt, we take the protection of our copyright and licenses very seriously. If you come across any illegal copies of our works, in any form, on the Internet, please provide us with the location address or website name immediately so that we can pursue a remedy.

Please contact us at copyright@packtpub.com with a link to the suspected pirated material.

We appreciate your help in protecting our authors, and our ability to bring you valuable content.

Questions

You can contact us at questions@packtpub.com if you are having a problem with any aspect of the book, and we will do our best to address it.

1
Building an Effective Intranet

One of the most common uses of SharePoint is as an organization's Intranet. While SharePoint has all of the critical ingredients within the platform to deliver a great solution, there is no out of the box template that delivers a complete solution. This often results in Intranet solutions that are underdeveloped and ineffective.

Building an effective Intranet starts with defining the overall goals and is followed by defining the information architecture, content and feature strategy, and user experience needed to support those goals. Common goals include the ability to deliver corporate communications, connect employees to increase collaboration, and to provide easy access to enterprise content and systems. Depending on the size, structure, and relative geography of users, those goals could translate to very different requirements.

This chapter will provide an overview of configuration steps needed to create an Intranet site, along with example customizations that can be created to provide dynamic and *relevant* content, which is a key ingredient to building an effective Intranet solution. The covered solutions include:

- Creating a Weather Web Part
- System status and notification features
- Building an Appropriate Use and Incident dialog
- Building an Employee Corner Web Part
- Building a Stock Ticker Web Part
- Content rollups

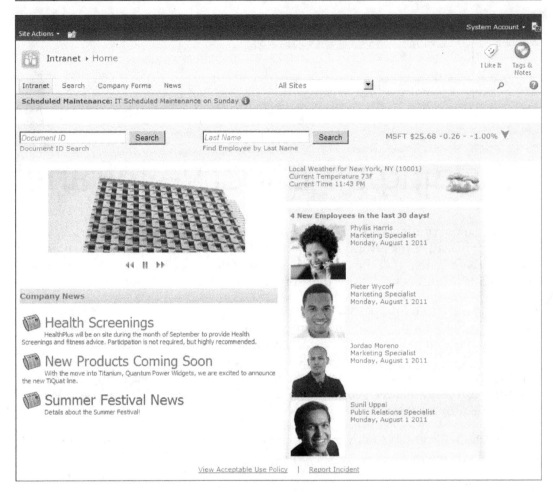

Preparing the Intranet site

It is important to set the right foundation for the Intranet site. It is easy to get lost in all of the options available, but this section will cover the design decisions behind choosing a site template, selecting which features to activate, and then selecting a page layout to support the landing page(s).

Choosing a site template

SharePoint ships with a number of site template options, but most of the templates were built for a very specific type purpose. When choosing a template for an Intranet site, it is best to select one of the more generic site options. The three to consider are:

- **Blank site**: A generic template that includes no lists or libraries. This is my first choice when building a top-level site collection such as this Intranet portal.

- **Team site**: A generic template that includes a standard site with commonly used lists and libraries including shared documents, calendar, and a discussions list.

- **Publishing template (SharePoint Server)**: A generic template that can be leveraged in large-scale publishing scenarios. The publishing template is by far the template that will require the most design work to get to a usable state, so therefore should only be used in this scenario if you have specific requirements for it. It is important to note that the publishing template is not required in order to leverage the publishing features. See the *Activating supporting features* section that follows.

A full overview of the available templates can be found on the Microsoft Office website at `http://office.microsoft.com/en-us/sharepoint-server-help/a-preview-of-the-sharepoint-server-2010-site-templates-HA101907564.aspx`

Activating supporting features

After choosing a site template and provisioning the site collection, the next step is to activate the initial features needed to support the Intranet site. The robust feature deployment and activation system supported in SharePoint makes it very easy to fine-tune the functionality available within a site. Since the available features vary depending on which version you are running (Foundation, Server Standard, and Server Enterprise), I will specify which version each feature ships with.

The following is a list of features activated on the site being configured for this book:

Site collection features		
Document ID service	SharePoint Server Standard and Enterprise	Assigns IDs to documents in the site collection, which can be used to retrieve items independent of their current location
Search Server Web Parts	SharePoint Server Standard and Enterprise	This feature uploads all Web Parts required for the Search Center
SharePoint Server Standard Site Collection features	SharePoint Server Standard and Enterprise	Features such as user profiles and search, included in SharePoint Server Standard License
SharePoint Server Enterprise Site Collection features	SharePoint Server Enterprise	Features such as InfoPath Forms Services, Visio Services, Access Services, and Excel Services Application
SharePoint Server Publishing Infrastructure	SharePoint Server Standard and Enterprise	Provides centralized libraries, content types, master pages and page layouts, and enables page scheduling and other publishing functionality for a site collection
Site features		
SharePoint Server Standard Site Collection features	SharePoint Server Standard and Enterprise	Features such as user profiles and search
SharePoint Server Enterprise Site Collection features	SharePoint Server Enterprise	Features such as InfoPath Forms Services, Visio Services, Access Services, and Excel Services Application
SharePoint Server Publishing Infrastructure	SharePoint Server Standard and Enterprise	Creates a web page library as well as supporting libraries to create and publish pages based on page layouts

For anyone that is not familiar with the publishing features, it is important to understand that the document libraries setup for publishing, including the resources provisioned when the feature is activated such as the Style Library, will require that all changes be fully published for non-administrators to be able to view the most recent changes. If changes are made to pages, scripts, images, or CSS stylesheets included in any of these libraries and are not fully published, you will see unexpected behaviors such as 404 errors, out of date content, or miscellaneous unexpected SharePoint page level errors relating to the item's status.

A full overview of the publishing features in SharePoint 2010 is available at http://technet.microsoft.com/en-us/library/ff628963.aspx

Selecting a layout

Then next step is to choose the high-level structure of the front page. The two default options are a standard home page or the new Wiki home page. While the Wiki home page offers some nice improvements over the standard home page formatting, a better option is to configure a new library to hold Web Part pages in order to leverage the configuration and security capabilities of a SharePoint document library.

 When using SharePoint Foundation where the publishing features are not available your options are limited to page level customizations using SharePoint Designer 2010.

With the publishing features activated on SharePoint Server Standard or Enterprise there are a number of layout options to consider. One of the important changes with SharePoint 2010 is that page layouts can now be changed, where previously they were set at the time the page was created and could not be changed later.

 It is important to note that if you change the layout, any Web Parts that are contained in a Web Part zone that no longer exists, will no longer be displayed and will need to be reapplied to the page.

After creating the library, create a page and select the **Page** tab. If this is going to be the home page for the site, be sure to click the **Make Homepage** button in the ribbon. The **Page Layout** option will be displayed in the ribbon, and clicking it will provide you thumbnails of the layout options as seen in the following screenshot:

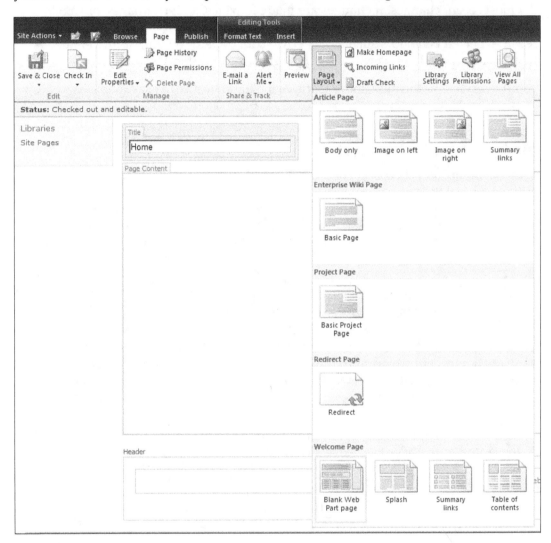

When choosing one of the layouts it is important to consider if you want the left hand navigation to be displayed or hidden. In scenarios where the left hand navigation is important I would select the **Blank Web Part page** layout under the **Welcome Page** grouping. In scenarios where you need more screen real estate or where the left hand navigation is not as important on the top-level site you can select the **Splash** layout. The **Splash** layout I have selected for this exercise is displayed in the following screenshot:

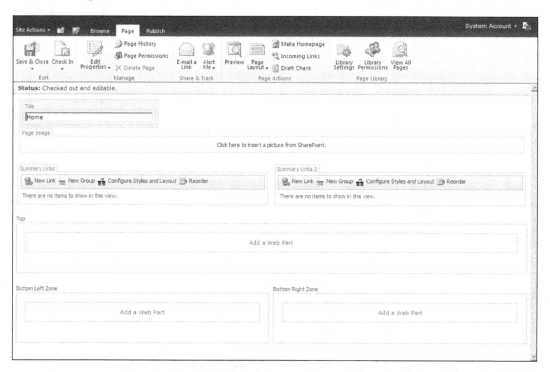

It is also possible to customize this layout if needed in SharePoint Designer, which may be preferable for simple changes instead of creating custom page layouts. It is important to note that editing page and page layouts directly with SharePoint Designer will put the item in an unghosted state which means that the page will no longer reference the common version of the item and instead store a version of the item in the content database that the site is stored in. This change will have a small impact on performance, but can also complicate future upgrades and should therefore be done with caution.

In the **Top Web Part Zone**, the default orientation is set to "Vertical", but for the page we are creating, it is more valuable set to "Horizontal" as shown in the following code snippet:

```
<WebPartPages:WebPartZone runat="server"
AllowPersonalization="false" ID="TopZone" FrameType="TitleBarOnly"
Title="<%$Resources:cms,WebPartZoneTitle_Top%>"
Orientation="Horizontal">
```

Downloading the example code

You can download the example code files for all Packt books you have purchased from your account at http://www.packtpub.com. If you purchased this book elsewhere, you can visit http://www.packtpub.com/support and register to have the files e-mailed directly to you.

To make the change perform the following steps:

1. Open the page layout in SharePoint Designer.
2. Locate the control with the ID "TopZone".
3. Change the orientation property from "Vertical" to "Horizontal".
4. Save the page layout.
5. Publish the page layout.

With the layout selected and the page set as the home page, we are now ready to start adding content.

Creating a Weather Web Part

In many organizations a frequent request is to display the current time and weather for one or more locations where the organization operates.

This exercise provides a great example of how to consume web based data to populate the content. For the purpose of this chapter I am going to consume a service provided by The Weather Channel ®. You will need to register as a partner in order to use this service. You can find additional details at http://portal.theweatherchannel.com/.

Approach

The easiest way to use this service is to load the content into the standard XML Web Part. This approach will also work in cloud-based environments such as Office 365. The **XML Viewer** Web Part is included under the **Content Rollup** category as displayed in the following screenshot:

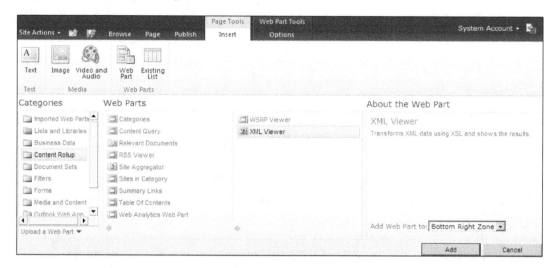

Configuring the XML Web Part

With the XML Web Part added to the page, configure the appearance properties such as title, height, and width. Set the XML link to the path of the service with the required inputs, and set the XSL link to the path of your XSL file. The best way to manage the XSL file is to upload it into a central style and script library on the site.

The contents of the XSL file should format the content into the desired format. The Weather.com web service will return a number of key attributes including the location, the current temperature, and the current time.

Weather Web Part displayed

A rendered version of the **Current Weather** Web Part is displayed in the following screenshot:

The standard SharePoint Web Parts can also be exported with configuration settings making it easy to reuse the content on many pages or sites. It can either be uploaded to the desired page(s) or added to the site collection's **Web Part Gallery**.

System status and notification features

Continuing the theme of using the Intranet as a communications mechanism, this next solution will leverage the Notification bar within SharePoint to communicate messages to users anywhere within the site. This is a great way to communicate topics like system status, organization news, or security bulletins.

The notification details will include a title, notification message, a category which will be used to change the notification background color and to display a corresponding image, as well as start and end dates in order to support scheduling to keep the content fresh and accurate.

This solution requires two parts:

- A list to manage the content
- Code embedded in the Master Page to handle the message retrieval and display

Notification List Definition and List Instance feature

We will provision a List Definition and List Instance to store the notification content. This will make it easy to reuse the list if necessary in cases where you need to manage the notifications separately for sites that target different sets of users or in different farms.

To create the feature perform the following steps:

1. Open Visual Studio 2010.

2. Select **File**, then **New Project**.

3. Browse the **Installed Templates** and select **Visual C# | SharePoint 2010**, and then **List Definition** as shown in the following screenshot:

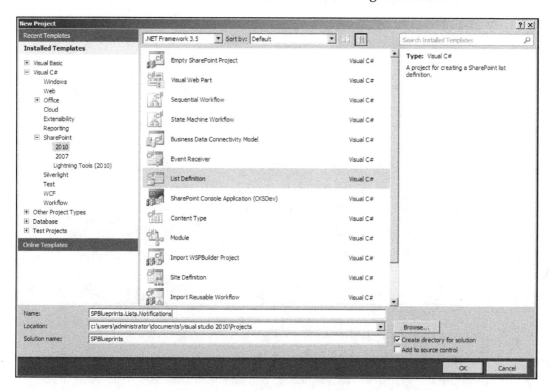

4. Enter the project details such as **Name**, **Location**, and **Solution name**.

5. Within the **SharePoint Customization Wizard**, provide a path to your SharePoint site and then be sure to select the option to **Deploy as a farm solution** as shown in the following screenshot:

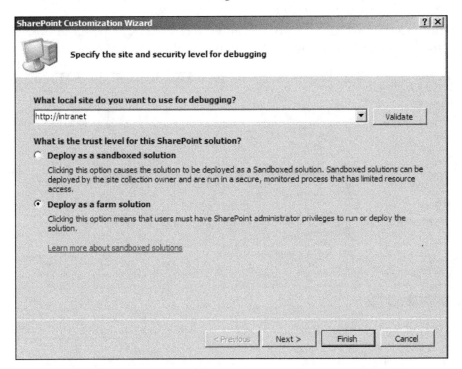

6. Rename the **ListDefinition1** item NotificationDefinition.
7. Rename the **ListInstance1** item Notification.
8. Rename the **Feature1** item SPBlueprints Notification List Feature.

9. Select the **SPBlueprints Notification List Feature.feature** item and provide a **Title** and **Description**. It should resemble the following screenshot:

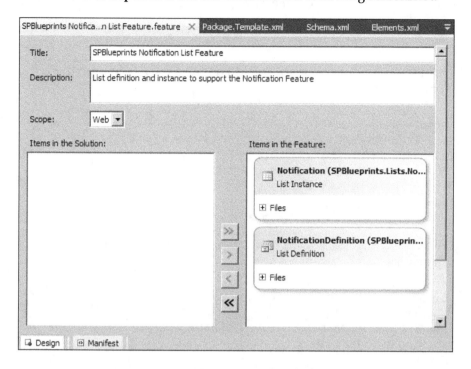

10. Next we will edit the `NotificationDefinition/Elements.xml` file to complete the List Definition. The `Elements.xml` file is used to describe the list and fields.

11. First, we will add in the field definitions. The following table provides a brief overview of the field element and attributes that we describe when defining a new field:

Attribute name	Description
Type	Used to describe which SharePoint field type will be used. Options include `Text`, `Choice`, `Decimal`, `URL`, and `DateTime`
DisplayName	The label that will be shown on forms and within the list views
Required	Boolean value that determines if it is a required field
MaxLength	If it is a `Text` field, the maximum number of characters allowed can be specified
ID	The unique ID or GUID used to identify the field
StaticName	The internal name of the field; this label cannot be changed and is set when the field is initially created

Attribute name	Description
Name	The name of the field
Group	The Group attribute is used for associating fields to make them easier to locate within the administration screens

12. For the Notification field, we will define a Text field with the following elements:

```
<Field Type="Text"
DisplayName="Notification"
Required="TRUE"
MaxLength="255"
ID="{6807197A-5A93-48D0-90B5-95DD0212ACDE}"
StaticName="Notification"
Name="Notification"
Group="Communication Columns" />
```

13. For the InfoLink field, we will define a URL field with the following elements:

```
<Field Type="URL"
DisplayName="Info Link"
Required="FALSE"
ID="{FEF259DC-8845-45E5-B9DB-578E905CA853}"
StaticName="InfoLink"
Name="InfoLink"
Group="Communication Columns" />
```

14. For the NotifStart field, we will define a simple DateTime field as follows:

```
<Field Type="DateTime"
DisplayName="Start Date"
Required="FALSE"
ID="{CD648248-7769-428C-955C-2E341A23848E}"
StaticName="NotifStart"
Name="NotifStart"
Group="Communication Columns" />
```

15. The NotifEnd field will be another DateTime field with the following elements:

```
<Field Type="DateTime"
DisplayName="End Date"
Required="FALSE"
ID="{0444ABD1-7E04-4EBF-9FF9-87061CA410F4}"
StaticName="NotifEnd"
Name="NotifEnd"
Group="Communication Columns" />
```

16. Next we define the attributes of the `ContentType` element, and set the field references to the IDs of the fields defined previously along with the standard `ID` field associated with the base content type item:

```
<ContentType
  ID="0x010089E3E6DB8C9B4B3FBB980447E313CE96"
  Name="Notification Item"
  Group="Communication Content Types"
  Description="Notification List Content Type."
  Version="0">
    <FieldRefs>
      <FieldRef ID="{fa564e0f-0c70-4ab9-b863-0177e6ddd247}" />
      <FieldRef ID="{6807197A-5A93-48D0-90B5-95DD0212ACDE}" />
      <FieldRef ID="{24380857-433E-4A73-BD71-16F3BB1E443D}" />
      <FieldRef ID="{CD648248-7769-428C-955C-2E341A23848E}" />
      <FieldRef ID="{0444ABD1-7E04-4EBF-9FF9-87061CA410F4}" />
      <FieldRef ID="{FEF259DC-8845-45E5-B9DB-578E905CA853}" />
    </FieldRefs>
</ContentType>
```

17. Next we will identify the attributes for the `ListTemplate` element, which completes the configuration for the new List Definition:

```
<ListTemplate
  Name="NotificationDefinition"
  DisallowContentTypes="FALSE"
  Type="12001"
  BaseType="0"
  OnQuickLaunch="FALSE"
  SecurityBits="11"
  Sequence="410"
  DisplayName="Notification List Definition"
  Description="Notification Definition"
  Image="/_layouts/images/itgen.png"/>
```

18. Edit the `NotificationDefinition/Notification/Elements.xml` file to set the configuration for the List Instance that will be provisioned:

```
<ListInstance Title="Notification"
  OnQuickLaunch="FALSE"
  TemplateType="12001"
  Url="Lists/Notification"
  Description="Notification List Instance">
</ListInstance>
```

19. To build the project, select **Build**, then **Build SPBlueprints.Lists. Notification**.

20. To deploy to the local server, select **Build**, then **Deploy SPBlueprints.Lists. Notification**.

21. The completed project structure should resemble the following screenshot:

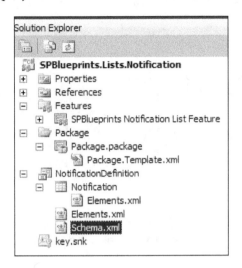

Notification list displayed

Since we are creating both a List Definition and a List Instance, the defined list will be automatically created once the SPBlueprints Notification List Feature is activated. It is important to note that the OnQuickLaunch property was set to FALSE so the list will not show up in the **Quick Launch** menu. To access the list you will need to click the **Site Actions** menu, and select the **View All Site Content** menu item.

The pre-defined list view also makes it easy for the content manager to review the currently logged notifications as shown in the following screenshot:

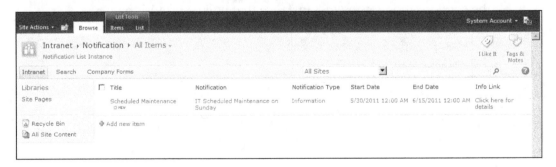

The **New Item** form includes the fields we defined in the List Definition, and can be used to log a variety of notifications as displayed in the following screenshot:

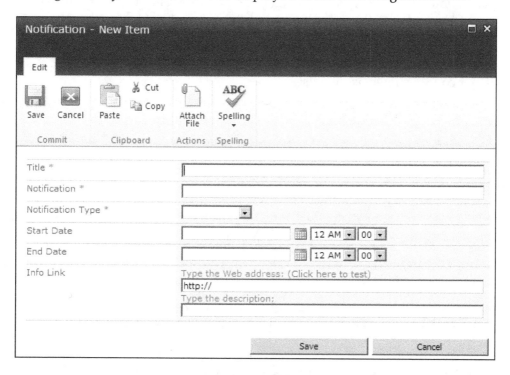

Presenting status notifications

To display notifications on the page we will query the Notification list we previously deployed, and leverage the SP.UI.Status class made available in the ECMA Client OM.

SP.UI.Status overview

The SP.UI.Status class supports a number of methods that allow you to add, update, append, and remove status messages as well as set a background color for the status bar. For the purpose of this particular feature, we will focus on the addStatus and setStatusPriColor functions.

Since this is part of the Client OM, it is accessible from any SharePoint page. The scripts can be added to a Content Editor Web Part, included in a custom Web Part, or as in this example added directly to the site's Master Page.

Adding SetStatus code to the Master Page

In this section we will add the `SetStatus` code to the Master Page for the status updates to be added to the page. It should be positioned just before the `</Body>` tag.

To start with, create a `div` container to hold the code and define the script block. The remainder of the code will be placed inside of the script block. The `SetStatus` script container code is shown as follows:

```
<div id="SetStatus">
  <script type="text/ecmascript" language="ecmascript">
  </script>
</div>
```

Next we define the main variables and add a check to determine if this is a page being loaded in a dialog window. This code is needed to prevent the status messages from being loaded in the dialog windows such as the file upload or edit item forms.

The `ExecuteOrDelayUntilScriptLoaded()` function will delay the execution of the script until the page and all scripts are loaded. The `SetStatus` variables and control code are shown as follows:

```
var statusId = '';
var isitDlg = window.location.href.match(/isDlg/i) != null;

if (!isitDlg) {
    ExecuteOrDelayUntilScriptLoaded(LoadNotifications, "sp.js");
}
```

The `LoadNotifications()` function will use the Client Object Model to format a CAML query, and load the matching items from the Notification list. The

`LoadNotifications()` function code is shown as follows:

```
function LoadNotifications() {
    var curDate = new Date();
    var curDFormatted = curDate.getYear() + "-" +
      (curDate.getMonth() + 1) + "-" + curDate.getDate() + "T" +
      curDate.getHours() + ":" + curDate.getMinutes() + ":" +
      curDate.getSeconds() + "Z";
    var listTitle = "Notification";
    context = SP.ClientContext.get_current();
    var notifList =
      context.get_web().get_lists().getByTitle(listTitle);
    var camlQuery = new SP.CamlQuery();
    camlQuery.set_viewXml("<View><Query><ViewFields><FieldRef
      Name='Title' /><FieldRef Name='Notification' /><FieldRef
```

```
       Name='NotifType' /><FieldRef Name='NotifStart' /><FieldRef
       Name='NotifEnd' /><FieldRef Name='InfoLink'
       /></ViewFields><Where><And><Leq><FieldRef Name='NotifStart'
       /><Value IncludeTimeValue='TRUE' Type='DateTime'>" +
       curDFormatted + "</Value></Leq><Geq><FieldRef Name='NotifEnd'
       /><Value IncludeTimeValue='TRUE' Type='DateTime'>" +
       curDFormatted +
       "</Value></Geq></And></Where><OrderBy><FieldRef
       Name='NotifStart' /></OrderBy></Query></View>");
    this.listItems = notifList.getItems(camlQuery);
    context.load(listItems);
    context.executeQueryAsync(ReadListItemSucceeded,
       ReadListItemFailed);
}
```

The `ReadListItemSucceeded()` function will be called if the list read call was successful. Here we will iterate through the returned items and format the status messages that will be displayed. The `ReadListItemSucceeded()` function code is shown as follows:

```
function ReadListItemSucceeded(sender, args) {
    var message = '';
    var items = listItems.getEnumerator();

    while (items.moveNext()) {
      var listItem = items.get_current();

        switch (listItem.get_item('NotifType')) {
          case "Emergency":
              imageRef = "<img
src='/_layouts/IMAGES/error16by16.gif' align='absmiddle'
border='0' alt='Emergency'>";
              break;
          case "Warning":
              imageRef = "<img
src='/_layouts/IMAGES/warning16by16.GIF' align='absmiddle'
border='0' alt='Warning'>";
              break;
          default:
              imageRef = "<img
src='/_layouts/IMAGES/info16by16.gif' align='absmiddle' border='0'
alt='Information'>";
        }
```

```
        message = listItem.get_item('Notification') + "      " +
    imageRef;
        SetStatus(listItem.get_item("Title") + ":", message,
          listItem.get_item('NotifType'));
    }
}
```

The `SetStatus()` function is called for each status message that needs to be set. It will use the `SP.UI.Status` methods to add a message and to set the background color of the status container. The `SetStatus()` function code is shown as follows:

```
function SetStatus(title, message, type) {
    statusId = SP.UI.Status.addStatus(title, message, false);

    switch (type) {
      case "Emergency":
          SP.UI.Status.setStatusPriColor(statusId, 'red');
          break;
      case "Warning":
          SP.UI.Status.setStatusPriColor(statusId, 'yellow');
          break;
      default:
          SP.UI.Status.setStatusPriColor(statusId, 'blue');
    }
}
```

The `ReadListItemFailed()` function will provide an alert if the status could not be set:

```
function ReadListItemFailed(sender, args) {
    alert('Error: ' + args.get_message());
}
```

Notifications displayed

The rendered version of the list driven notification system is shown in the following screenshot. If multiple notices are returned, each will be displayed on a separate line.

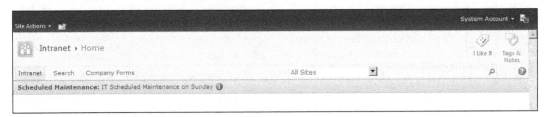

Building an Appropriate Use and Incident dialog

Next we will extend our solution and show an easy way to provide global links as part of the standard footer in the Master Page. While the linked content can be to anything web accessible, the sample solution will be used to link to an appropriate use page as well as a form used for reporting content.

Many environments today are investing time and effort into creating a SharePoint Governance Plan, or have existing Appropriate Use or Information Security policies. Creating a policy is relatively easy, but making it easy to find and access is something that many organizations struggle with. It is also critical to provide easily accessible incident reporting mechanisms so that the system can be self-policed as much as possible.

Approach

Since this is content we want to display globally, we are going to include it as part of the standard footer in the Master Page. This will guarantee that it is easily accessible. For the presentation, I think this is a good use of the Client OM's SP.UI.Dialog class which creates an Ajax shadowbox.

To simplify the example, we will use a standard SharePoint Survey list for the Incident Report form. You could alternatively create an application page and deploy it to the farm.

Showing the form

We are going to start by adding the div container govFooter to the Master Page, just above the <SharePoint:DeveloperDashboard runat="server"/> control. The remainder of the code will be placed inside this container. We will reference the stylesheet class s4-notdlg which has special meaning within SharePoint. When this class is referenced, it will ensure that this content will be hidden from any dialog windows, such as the ones we are launching with the code added in this section:

```
<div id="govFooter" class="s4-notdlg" style=" text-align:center;
  width:100%">
  <script type="text/ecmascript">

  </script>
</div>
```

Calling the modal dialog is as easy as calling the `showModalDialog()` function, and passing it the input options for what to display. The `showPolicy()` and `showIncidentForm()` functions are as follows:

```
function showPolicy() {
var _options = { url: "http://intranet/Pages/Acceptable-Use-
Policy.aspx", width: "800", title: "Appropriate Use Policy" };
SP.UI.ModalDialog.showModalDialog(_options);
}

function showIncidentForm() {
var _options = { url:
"http://intranet/Lists/Incident%20Reports/NewForm.aspx", width:
"800", title: "Report Incident" };
SP.UI.ModalDialog.showModalDialog(_options);
}
```

Next we just have to call the two functions with a JavaScript function call added to an anchor tag:

```
<a href="javascript:showPolicy();" style="text-
  decoration:underline">View Acceptable Use Policy</a>
   |   
<a href="javascript:showIncidentForm();" style="text-
  decoration:underline">Report Incident</a>
```

Appropriate Use and Incident dialog displayed

The standard footer linking to the Appropriate Use Policy and the Incident Report dialog is represented in the following screenshot:

View Acceptable Use Policy | Report Incident

The **Appropriate Use Policy** dialog is represented in the following screenshot:

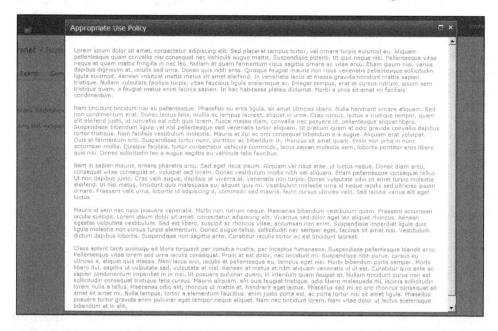

The **Incident Report** dialog is represented in the following screenshot:

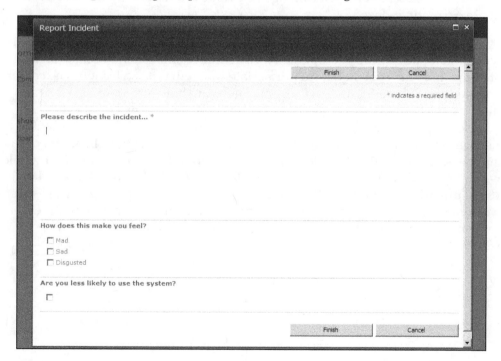

Building an Employee Corner Web Part

Highlighting employees is a great way to increase collaboration and user engagement. In the past this was done in employee newsletters or other communication methods, but as those methods go electronic and the focus moves towards the Intranet portal as the central communication hub, it becomes another type of information that should be included.

 SharePoint Server's user profiles can provide a rich set of details about users, and can be leveraged to provide a great source of dynamic content around important dates, organization structure, interests, clients, and past projects.

The Employee Corner Web Part will present a list of new employees based on the Hire Date field in the user profiles. Additional examples could include employee of the month (or quarter), birth dates, or employee anniversaries.

Approach

To create the Employee Corner Web Part we will create a custom Web Part in Visual Studio 2010. The Web Part will leverage the Search API's `FullTextSqlQuery` class to query the People search scope bringing back values stored within the user profiles that are currently indexed.

It is important to understand the underlying architecture in order to know which development path is really an option. Normal SharePoint list and library data is stored inside of the content database associated with the site collection. The content associated with SharePoint's service applications are however stored in separate databases since those services and the content is not tied to any one site, but available globally to all web applications associated with the service application. This means that the service applications are not accessible via the Client OM or via Sandbox Solutions without implementing some sort of Full Trust proxy that would have to be installed on the server and provide access to the server API. Based on these boundaries, a server solution makes the best choice for the approach in most environments. If the solution needs to be deployed to an environment with server deployment limitations the Full Trust proxy or other alternatives would have to be evaluated.

Creating the Web Part

To create the initial project:

1. Open Visual Studio 2010.

2. Select **File**, then **New Project**.

3. Browse the **Installed Templates** and select **Visual C# | SharePoint 2010**, and then **Empty SharePoint Project** as shown in the following screenshot:

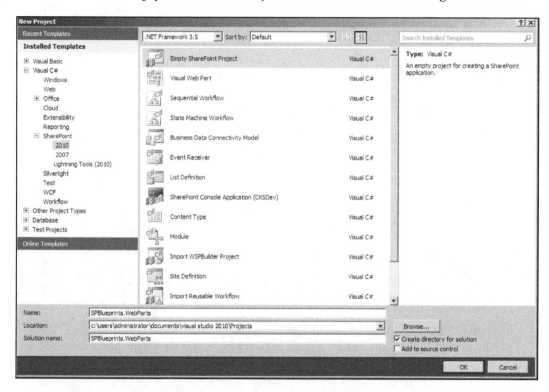

4. Enter the project details such as **Name, Location,** and **Solution name.**

5. Within the **SharePoint Customization Wizard**, provide a path to your SharePoint site and then be sure to select the option to **Deploy as a farm solution** as shown in the following screenshot:

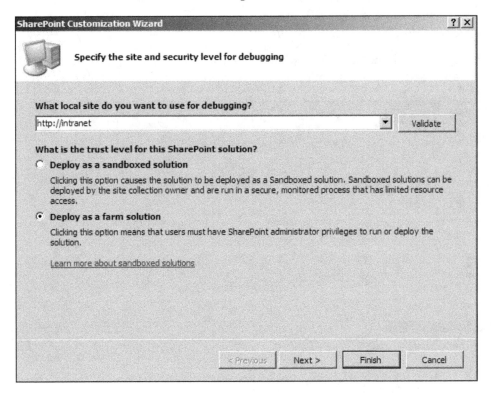

6. Right-click on the project file and select **Add New Item**.
7. From the template selection screen select the **Web Part** option.

8. Provide the name `EmployeeCorner` and click the **Add** button as illustrated in the following screenshot:

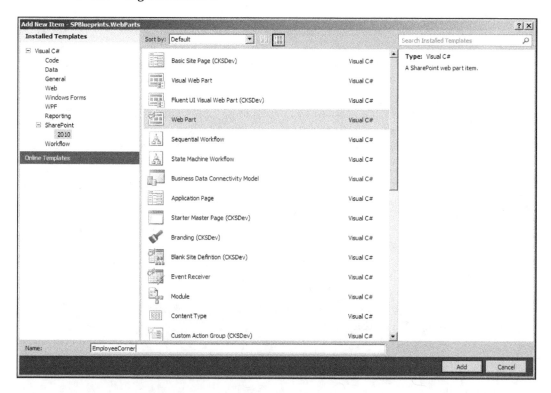

9. Rename the **Feature1** item `SPBlueprints.WebParts`.

10. Select the `SPBlueprints.WebParts` feature item and provide a **Title** and **Description**. It should resemble the following screenshot:

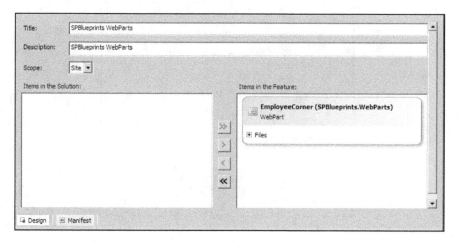

11. Edit the definition of the `EmployeeCorner.webpart` file so that the Web Part definition added to the **Gallery** is meaningful as displayed in the following `EmployeeCorner.webpart` definition:

```xml
<?xml version="1.0" encoding="utf-8"?>
<webParts>
  <webPart xmlns="http://schemas.microsoft.com/WebPart/v3">
    <metaData>
      <type
name="SPBlueprints.WebParts.EmployeeCorner.EmployeeCorner,
$SharePoint.Project.AssemblyFullName$" />
<importErrorMessage>$Resources:core,ImportErrorMessage;</import
ErrorMessage>
    </metaData>
    <data>
      <properties>
        <property name="Title" type="string">Employee
Corner</property>
        <property name="Description" type="string">SPBlueprints
- The Employee Corner WebPart displays all new employees that
started in the last 30 days.</property>
    <property name="SearchProxyName" type="string">Search
Service Application</property>
      </properties>
    </data>
  </webPart>
</webParts>
```

12. The completed project structure should resemble the following screenshot:

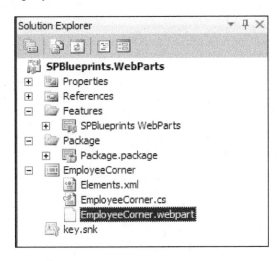

Defining a Web Part property

When creating a Web Part, there is often some configuration data that is needed to be able to reuse the Web Part for different sites or purposes. Creating a Web Part property makes it much easier to maintain the code than embedding configuration values in the code.

For the `EmployeeCorner` Web Part, we are going to establish a text field that allows the user to specify the Search service application to use when searching for the user profiles in the next section. The `SearchProxyName` property is detailed as follows:

```
private string searchProxyName;

[WebBrowsable(true),
 WebDisplayName("Search Proxy Name"),
 WebDescription("Please provide the name of your Search Service
Application."),
 Personalizable(PersonalizationScope.Shared)]
 public string SearchProxyName
 {
   get { return searchProxyName; }
   set { searchProxyName = value; }
 }
```

Connecting to the Search service application

To work with the Search service application we need to start by adding a reference to the following namespaces within the project and `EmployeeCorner` Web Part:

```
Microsoft.SharePoint.Administration
Microsoft.Office.Server.Search
Microsoft.Office.Server.Search.Query
Microsoft.Office.Server.Search.Administration
```

The connection to the service application is established through the `SearchServiceApplicationProxy` object, which is loaded using the `SearchProxyName` Web Part property previously identified. The following code should be added to a new method called `Display()` that is called from the `OnLoad()` method:

```
SearchQueryAndSiteSettingsServiceProxy settingsProxy =
SPFarm.Local.ServiceProxies.GetValue<SearchQueryAndSiteSettingsSer
viceProxy>();
SearchServiceApplicationProxy searchProxy =
settingsProxy.ApplicationProxies.GetValue<SearchServiceApplication
Proxy>(this.searchProxyName);
FullTextSqlQuery mQuery = new FullTextSqlQuery(searchProxy);
```

The `FullTextSqlQuery` class provides an interface to execute complex queries against the search index. Queries executed against the index will perform faster than queries against the actual content such as a list or a library. As the amount of content increases, and as the number content sources you search across increases, the performance gains are even more significant, since the index provides a pre-processed source for the information.

For the `FullTextSqlQuery`, we will define the fields that we want to see, the scope, and the criteria to match it. For the fields you will want to make sure that the desired fields are set up as **Managed Properties**. The name of a Managed Property may be different than the name in the actual profile. In this example, the user profile field's internal name is `SPS-HireDate`, but the Managed Property name is simply `HireDate`. You can check the Managed Property mappings within the Search service application by clicking the **Metadata Properties** link in the Quick Launch menu.

For any search involving people, it is required that you use the People search scope so that it returns user profile information instead of regular site content. The New Hire Query will pull the specified fields, from the People search scope, for anyone with a `HireDate` that is within 30 days of today. An example of the query is shown as follows:

```
mQuery.QueryText = "SELECT LastName, FirstName, JobTitle,
accountname, HireDate, Birthday, PictureThumbnailURL FROM SCOPE()
WHERE (\"scope\" = 'People') AND HireDate >= DATEADD (DAY, -30,
GETGMTDATE())";
```

After setting the query, there are a few other properties that need to be set before executing the query, which are shown as follows:

```
mQuery.ResultTypes = ResultType.RelevantResults;
mQuery.TrimDuplicates = true;
mQuery.RowLimit = 100;
ResultTableCollection resultNew = mQuery.Execute();
```

Formatting the Web Part

Formatting the output of the Web Part begins with identifying any controls that are needed within the `CreateChildControls()` method. This method will run as part of the initialization process before the `OnLoad()` method, ensuring the controls are available. The output that will be rendered, will be added to the literal control. The `CreateChildControls()` method code is shown as follows:

```
protected override void CreateChildControls()
{
  this.literalMessage = new Literal();
  this.literalMessage.ID = "literalMessage";
```

```
        this.Controls.Add(this.literalMessage);
    }
```

Within the `Display()` method, after the `Execute()` method previously called, we will now process the results. When executing a search query, the resulting `ResultsTableCollection` contains a number of different types of results. For the content that will be displayed here, we are interested in the `ResultType.RelevantResults`. We will check to validate that there are records returned, then extract just the relevant results.

Content that will be rendered to the screen will be formatted in a `StringBuilder` object called `messages`. After the main content is structured, we will iterate through the `DataTable` object to add each of the individual records returned from the query. The code is shown as follows:

```
DataTable resultsNewHire = new DataTable();
if (resultNew.Count > 0)
{
  ResultTable relevantResults =
  resultNew[ResultType.RelevantResults];
  resultsNewHire.Load(relevantResults,
   LoadOption.OverwriteChanges);
  messages.AppendFormat(@"<table width='360' border='0'
  cellpadding='0' cellspacing='0'><tr><td align='left'
   valign='top' width='14' class='ms-wpTdSpace'
   background='/Style%20Library/Images/shadow-
   left.png'> </td><td
   background='/Style%20Library/Images/mid-
   background.jpg'><table><tr><td colspan='2' class='ms-
   standardheader ms-WPTitle'><b>{0} New Employees in the last 30
   days!</b></td></tr>", resultsNewHire.Rows.Count);
  foreach (DataRow row in resultsNewHire.Rows)
  {
    messages.AppendFormat(@"<tr valign='center'><td width='100'><a
    href='/my/person.aspx?Accountname={3}'><img src='{5}' alt='{1}
    {0}' border='0'></a></td><td width='250' align='left'
    valign='top'><a href='/my/person.aspx?Accountname={3}'>{1}
    {0}</a><br>{2}<br>{4}</a></td></tr>", row[0].ToString(),
    row[1].ToString(), row[2].ToString(), row[3].ToString(),
    String.Format("{0:dddd, MMMM d yyyy}", row[4]),
    row[6].ToString());
  }
  messages.AppendFormat(@"</table></td><td align='right'
  valign='top' width='14' class='ms-wpTdSpace'
  background='http://intranet/Style%20Library/Images/shadow-
  right.png'> </td></tr></table>");
}
```

Employee Corner Web Part displayed

The rendered version of the Employee Corner Web Part is shown in the following screenshot:

Building a Stock Ticker Web Part

For publicly traded companies it is also desirable to display the current stock quote information. Like the Weather Web Part previously configured, there are many publicly available services that can provide this information. For this example, we will query a REST based service provided by Yahoo having the following address:

```
http://query.yahooapis.com/v1/public/yql?q=select * from yahoo.
finance.quotes where symbol in ("MSFT")&env=store://datatables.org/
alltableswithkeys
```

Approach

The stock quote information can be shown in a number of different ways. In cases where the information needs to be on every page, it should be added to a container on the Master Page with the s4-notdlg style reference previously included in the *Building an Appropriate Use and Incident dialog* section. For this example though, we will include it as an XML Web Part configured in a similar way to the Weather Web Part previously reviewed.

```
<?xml version="1.0" encoding="utf-8"?>
<xsl:stylesheet version="1.0"
xmlns:xsl="http://www.w3.org/1999/XSL/Transform"
xmlns:msxsl="urn:schemas-microsoft-com:xslt" exclude-result-
prefixes="msxsl">
  <xsl:output method="html" indent="yes"/>
  <xsl:template name="main">
    <xsl:variable name="symbol" select="results/quote/Symbol"/>
    <xsl:variable name="price"
     select="results/quote/LastTradePriceOnly"/>
    <xsl:variable name="change"
     select="results/quote/Change_PercentChange"/>
    <div id="stockInfo" style="font-size:10pt">
      <xsl:value-of select="$symbol" />
      <xsl:text> $</xsl:text>
      <xsl:value-of select="$price" />
      <xsl:text> </xsl:text>
      <xsl:value-of select="$change" />
      <xsl:text> </xsl:text>
      <xsl:choose>
        <xsl:when test="contains($change,'+')" >
          <img
src="http://intranet/Style%20Library/Images/stock_up.png"
border="0" alt="Trending Up"></img>
        </xsl:when>
        <xsl:otherwise>
          <img
src="http://intranet/Style%20Library/Images/stock_down.png"
border="0" alt="Trending Down"></img>
        </xsl:otherwise>
      </xsl:choose>
    </div>
  </xsl:template>
  <xsl:template match="/*">
    <xsl:call-template name="main"/>
  </xsl:template>
</xsl:stylesheet>
```

Stock Quote Web Part displayed

A rendered version of the current Stock Ticker Web Part can be displayed in the following screenshot:

MSFT $27.53 +0.435 - +1.61% ▲

Content rollups

An important part of developing a content strategy is to plan where content will be stored and where it needs to be displayed. In many cases content will be displayed in multiple locations or aggregated with other content. These aggregated content sources are often called content rollups and they provide a great way to reuse content throughout your SharePoint environment.

Approach

There are three common ways to aggregate content to create a content rollup:

- Content Query Web Part (CQWP)
- Search Web Parts
- Custom Web Parts

Let's review each of these options in more detail.

Content Query Web Part (CQWP)

The first is to use one of SharePoint's standard Web Parts like the **Content Query Web Part (CQWP)** that comes with SharePoint Server. Using the CQWP, it is possible to configure a query rule that will look for content in all sites within the site collection, within site below a selected site, or within a specified list or library. The query configuration also allows you to specify which list type and content type to query for. This allows you to cast a pretty wide net and pull back the related content. It also underscores the importance of properly classifying your content so that it can be easily identified. There are also a number of presentation properties that can be configured to present the content in different ways.

There are two serious limitations to the CQWP, the first is that it may not perform very well in very large sites or in aggregating large lists of content. It is important to understand that when a page is loaded with the CQWP, it will issue the requests to go grab the content. This can be a very expensive call requiring significant processing power from the server. There is some caching available, but it may not be effective enough with large sets of data. The second limitation is with the presentation options available. It is very easy to configure the presentation, but if one of the available options does not meet your needs it is not possible to have full control over the presentation.

For the purpose of this exercise the content is pretty simple so we will configure the rollup using the CQWP.

Search Web Parts

Utilizing the search system has distinct advantage that the information in the search index is optimized to return results significantly faster than querying the content sources. In addition, you have the ability to pull content from additional site collections or content sources within the search index. Using the Search Core Results Web Part you can specify a moderately complex query, the properties you need, and then the output can be fully customized by supplying custom XSL to format the returned XML.

The downside to using the search features is that the content has to be indexed for it to be available for display. Depending on the crawl frequency there is content that could be excluded, and typically the most recent content is the most relevant.

For a demonstration of using the Search Web Parts to aggregate content, see *Chapter 4, Building an Engaging Community Site* which will use the Search Web Parts to dynamically display people and content.

Custom Web Part

When developing a custom Web Part you have full control over how the content is pulled as well as how it is presented which gives you the best of all options. You have the option of either querying the source data or the search index, and you also have the ability to take advantage of advanced caching techniques which is valuable for highly trafficked pages.

The only downside to this approach is that it takes a lot more time and effort to build and test the customization than to configure the previously mentioned Web Parts. Also, in environments where farm solutions cannot be deployed to the server, this may not be an option.

For a demonstration of using more advanced techniques within a custom Web Part, see *Chapter 3, Building an Enterprise Content Management Solution*, which will leverage a series of custom Web Parts to aggregate form submissions.

Creating the content source

For the purpose of this exercise a simple subsite was created called News. Articles will be published to the **Site Pages** library on that site. To make the content easy to identify, a new content type was created called News, which inherits from the Article Page content type. The Article Page, and therefore the News content type has a number of properties that allow you to identify a number of pieces of metadata including By Line, Scheduling Start Date, Scheduling End Date, Article Date, and Rollup Image which will be used in the presentation of the rollup information. In addition, an additional Summary field can be added to provide some additional content.

Configuring the Content Query Web Part

To start with, **Edit** the **Page** and add the **Content Query** Web Part to the **Page**. It is available under the **Content Rollup** category as displayed in the following screenshot:

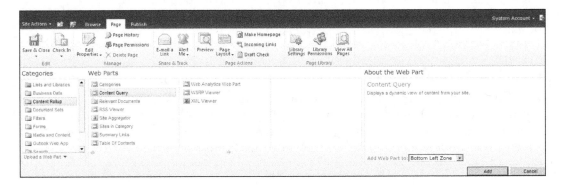

The next step is to configure the source of the content. To query for content within the entire site collection you can keep the default setting as **Show items from all sites in this site collection**. If the site is large, or you only want to look in specific locations, you can select one of the other options that narrow the scope. A list of the **Source** options are shown in the following screenshot:

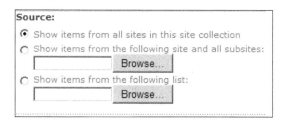

Next you define what types of items to display by setting the **List Type** value, along with the **Content Type**, as displayed in the following screenshot:

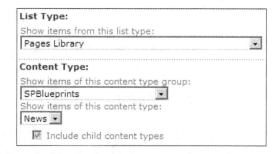

You also have the option of further filtering based on the property metadata that is available. This can be helpful to pinpoint the most valuable content within the system. In this case we are going to filter on the **Scheduling End Date** field and look for items with a date that is less than or equal to today, as seen in the following screenshot:

For the presentation configuration you have the ability to determine Group By, Sorting, and Item Limit information similar to a list view.

The **Styles** section has the most impact on how the content is presented, because it is used to select the associated XSL used to format the content for the page. For the headline with summary option we have chosen the **Large title Item style** as displayed in the following screenshot:

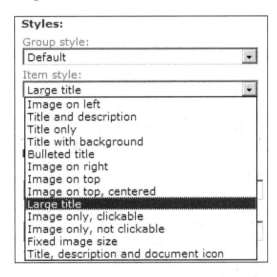

Next we need to map the list properties to the standard CQWP fields. In the case of the News article example we will stick pretty close to the default values, and only modify the **Description** field to include the **Summary** field we added to the News content type as displayed in the following screenshot:

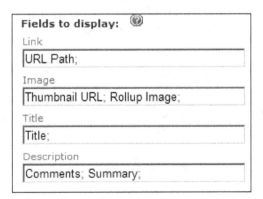

News content rollup displayed

Once configured this will pull and display any items added to the site collection
with the News content type and display them until after the scheduled end date
has passed. Newest articles will be displayed at the top of the list. The News content
rollup is displayed in the following screenshot:

Company News

 Health Screenings

HealthPlus will be on site during the month of September to provide Health Screenings and fitness advice. Participation is
not required, but highly recommended.

 New Products Coming Soon

With the move into Titanium, Quantum Power Widgets, we are excited to announce the new TiQuat line.

Summer Festival News

Details about the Summer Festival!

Summary

This section leveraged both the Server and Client OMs to create both packaged
and unpackaged solutions in order to deliver the overall business solution. The
customizations are grouped as follows:

- Browser-based configuration:
    - Provision a site collection: Create a new site collection used to hold
      our solution
    - Activate features: Activate the features needed to support our
      Intranet publishing solution
    - Selecting a page layout: Provides an overview of the available page
      layout options and details on how to change the page layout
    - Configuring an XML Web Part: Utilize the XML Web Part to call a
      web service and format the output for display
    - Create a List Instance: Provision new lists for storing content within
      our site collection
    - Content Query Web Part (CQWP): Configure the CQWP to display a
      roll up of the most recent news for display on our main splash page

- Visual Studio 2010:

    ○ Creating a List Definition

    ○ Create a List Instance: Create an instance of our custom list

    ○ Create a custom Web Part: Create a custom Web Part to display new employees

    ○ User profiles: Used to store information about the system users and leveraged by the Employee Corner Web Part

    ○ Search API: Used to provide a list of new employees to the Employee Corner Web Part

- SharePoint Designer 2010:

    ○ Master Page customization: Add new content and scripts to the Master Page so that they can be leveraged wherever the Master Page is applied

    ○ Page layout customization: Customize the page layout to add or configure controls

    ○ Page customization: Add new Web Parts or customize the Web Part zone properties

    ○ Dialog framework: Utilize the Client OM's `ModelDialog` methods to display standardized Ajax shadowboxes

These solutions provide examples of how to extend the out of the box features to build an effective Intranet site that excels at communicating important information, connecting people to build relationships, and expand on collaboration practices. In addition to implementing these solutions, they can also be adapted for other types of content to provide similar solutions.

2
Building an Out of Office Delegation Solution

For organizations looking to leverage SharePoint to support collaboration and process automation, it is important to be able to provide a more robust Out of Office solution than what is available within messaging systems like Microsoft Exchange. Those solutions do a good job of providing information that aligns with the user's current status, but it is not something that can be used to automate the delegation or assignment of tasks to ensure that processes continue to complete in a timely manner, while the user is unavailable. The lack of timely responses is one of the biggest challenges with most process automation projects, and it is not enough just to know who the task is currently assigned to.

A variation of this solution could also be used to provide a standing long term delegation for cases such as when a manager wants to delegate all tasks to a subordinate. This general process could be used to log the delegation in the log for compliance, while still assigning the task to the person who will actually do the work.

This chapter will provide the blueprints for a solution that leverages the user profiles with custom user properties.

The following solutions will be created:

- **Master Delegation Log**: A custom List Definition and List Instance to store delegation information centrally
- **Out of Office delegation workflow activity**: A custom full-trust workflow action to manage the delegation check and logging
- **Sample workflow**: A sample workflow that utilizes the Out of Office delegation workflow activity

- **Out of Office delegation Web Part**: A custom Web Part to display the delegation information
- **View Delegation History page**: An application page that displays the relevant delegation history

User profile properties

The user profiles available in SharePoint Server provide a robust set of features to centrally store and manage information about users. Custom fields can be easily configured to support your industry, organization, or business processes in the case of the Out of Office delegation solution.

To configure the user profile properties, navigate to the **User Profile Service Application** within **Central Administration**, and select the **Manage User Properties** link under the **People** group as shown in the following screenshot:

From the **Manage User Properties** page you can view the listing of all categories and properties as displayed in the following screenshot. The properties can be ordered as desired to provide logical groupings.

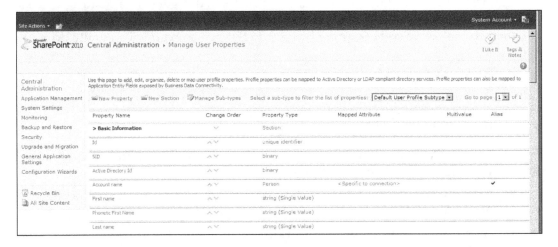

Defining the section and properties

For this solution we are going to define a section and three properties to support the Out of Office delegation.

To create a new section:

1. Click on the **New Section** menu item.
2. Provide the **Name** (internal name) as OutOfOffice.
3. Provide the **Display Name** as Out of Office Delegation.
4. Click on the **OK** button.

To create the Out of Office start date profile property:

1. Click on the **New Property** menu item.
2. Set the value for the **Name** field to outStartDate.
3. Set the value for the **Display Name** field to Out of Office Start Date.
4. Set the value for the **Type** field to **Date**.
5. Ensure that the **Default User Profile Subtype** is set to the **Yes** value.
6. Set the value for the **Description** field to Start Date for Delegating Out of Office task assignments.
7. Set the value for the **Policy Setting** field to **Optional**.
8. Set the value for the **Edit Settings** field to **Allow users to edit values for this property**.
9. Set the value for the **Show in the Profile properties section** field to Yes.
10. Set the value for the **Show on Edit Details** page to **Yes**.

To create the out of office end date profile property:

1. Click on the **New Property** menu item.
2. Set the value for the **Name** field to outEndDate.
3. Set the value for the **Display Name** field to Out of Office End Date.
4. Set the value for the **Type** field to **Date**.
5. Ensure that the **Default User Profile Subtype** is set to the **Yes** value.
6. Set the value for the **Description** field to End Date for Delegating Out of Office task assignments.
7. Set the value for the **Policy Setting** field to **Optional**.
8. Set the value for the **Edit Settings** field to **Allow users to edit values for this property**.
9. Set the value for the **Show in the Profile properties section** field to Yes.
10. Set the value for the **Show on Edit Details** page to **Yes**.

To create the out of office delegate profile property:

1. Click on the **New Property** menu item.

2. Set the value for the **Name** field to `outDelegation`.

3. Set the value for the **Display Name** field to `Out of Office Delegate`.

4. Set the value for the **Type** field to **Person**.

5. Ensure that the **Default User Profile Subtype** is set to the **Yes** value.

6. Set the value for the **Description** field to `Person to assign new workflow tasks to`.

7. Set the value for the **Policy Setting** field to **Optional**.

8. Set the value for the **Edit Settings** field to **Allow users to edit values for this property**.

9. Set the value for the **Show in the Profile properties section** field to **Yes**.

10. Set the value for the **Show on Edit Details** page to **Yes**.

Populating the properties

There are two different ways to edit the user profile properties for a user through the UI. For any property configured to appear and be editable on the **Edit Details** screen, the user or an administrator can browse to the user profile page and click on the **Edit My Profile** link as seen in the following user profile page screenshot. From there, make the desired changes and then click on the **Save and Close** menu item available at both the top and bottom of the page.

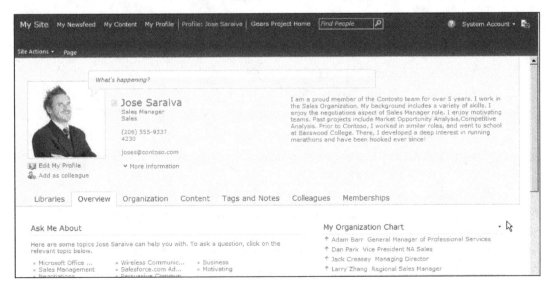

Alternatively the administrator can edit any profile, and all editable properties, from the **User Profile Service Application** by selecting the **Manage User Properties** menu item as displayed in the following screenshot:

From here you can search for the user profile you would like to edit, and then select the **Edit My Profile** option from the item menu as displayed in the following screenshot:

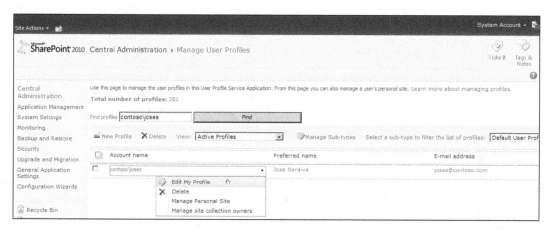

All available fields will be shown on the administrator version of the edit user profile form available from **Central Administration**. Once the required changes are made, simply click on the **Save and Close** menu item at the top or bottom of the page.

Test data will be needed in order to complete and test the remainder of the components of this solution, so be sure to have some user accounts available with and without out of office data.

While it is not needed for this solution, it is possible to do bulk updates to the user profile properties via profile import, custom code, or PowerShell. This can be helpful when defining new properties and the value of those properties are already stored in another system. Automatically importing or updating those property values will remove the need for the user to edit those values themselves.

Master Delegation Tracking List

To support compliance and reporting capabilities we will define a custom list that can be used for logging all of the delegation entries in a central list. This list can also be used to show a user what tasks were delegated on their behalf as we will see when we define the View Delegation History page referenced from the Task Delegation Web Part.

Delegation List Definition and List Instance

We will provision a List Definition and List Instance to store the notification content. This will make it easy to reuse the list, if necessary, in cases where you need to manage the notifications separately for sites that target different sets of users or in different farms.

To create the feature:

1. Open Visual Studio 2010.
2. Select **File**, then **New Project**.
3. Browse the **Installed Templates** and select **Visual C#, SharePoint 2010**, and then **List Definition** as seen in the following screenshot:

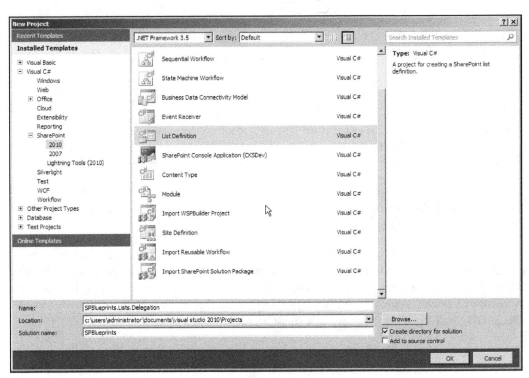

4. Enter the project details such as **Name**, **Location**, and **Solution name**.

5. Within the **SharePoint Customization Wizard**, provide a path to your SharePoint site and then be sure to select the option to **Deploy as a farm solution** as seen in the following screenshot:

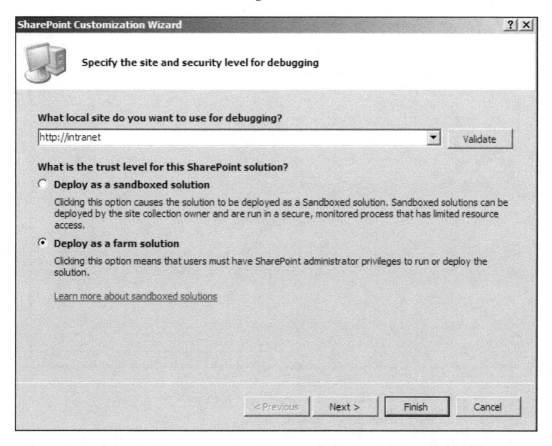

6. Provide a display name for the List Definition, select the **Custom List** type, and click on the **Finish** button as shown in the following screenshot:

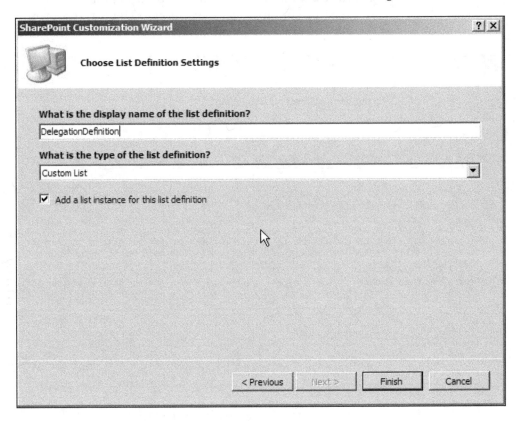

7. Rename the **ListDefinition1** item as `DelegationDefinition`.

8. Rename the **ListInstance1** item as `Delegation`.

9. Edit the `DelegationDefinition/Elements.xml` file and add in the content for `Elements.xml`.

10. For the `SiteName` field we would define a `Text` field with the following elements:

```
<Field Type="Text"
 DisplayName="Site Name"
 Required="TRUE"
 MaxLength="255"
 ID="{F0A3BFF6-F8F9-40E2-8031-2FEFD66FE8F3}"
 StaticName="SiteName"
 Name="SiteName"
 Group="Compliance Columns" />
```

11. For the `ListName` field we would define a `Text` field with the following elements:

```
<Field Type="Text"
 DisplayName="List Name"
 Required="TRUE"
 ID="{F6057985-C41D-4A30-8342-FF4E815BA51F}"
 StaticName="ListName"
 Name="ListName"
 Group="Compliance Columns" />
```

12. For the `WorkflowName` field we would define a `Text` field with the following elements:

```
<Field Type="Text"
 DisplayName="Workflow Name"
 Required="TRUE"
 ID="{4B57EC1E-C6CD-4197-ABEF-81754013DDD4}"
 StaticName="WorkflowName"
 Name="WorkflowName"
 Group="Compliance Columns" />
```

13. For the `OrigUser` field we would define a `User` field with the following elements:

```
<Field Type="User"
 DisplayName="Original User"
 Required="TRUE"
 ID="{68C1C89A-324D-48C3-AB1E-26AA7003A37F}"
 StaticName="OrigUser"
 Name="OrigUser"
 Group="Compliance Columns" />
```

14. For the `DelegUser` field we would define a `User` field with the following elements:

```
<Field Type="User"
 DisplayName="Delegate User"
 Required="TRUE"
 ID="{83856973-C1B3-401A-8687-52633D8B2ADC}"
 StaticName="DelegUser"
 Name="DelegUser"
 Group="Compliance Columns" />
```

15. For the `LogDate` field we would define a `DateTime` field with the following elements:

```
<Field Type="DateTime"
 DisplayName="Log Date"
 Required="FALSE"
 ID="{EF890C5F-0DE6-44D6-B994-BC269E830E0E}"
 StaticName="LogDate"
 Name="LogDate"
 Group="Compliance Columns" />
```

16. Next we define the attributes of the content type and set the field references to the IDs of the fields defined in the previous steps, along with the standard `ID` field associated with the base content type item:

```
<ContentType
 ID="0x010089E3E6DB8C9B4B3FBB980447E313CE97"
 Name="Delegation Log Entry"
 Group="Compliance Content Types"
 Description="Delegation Log Content Type."
 Version="0">
  <FieldRefs>
    <FieldRef ID="{fa564e0f-0c70-4ab9-b863-0177e6ddd247}" />
    <FieldRef ID="{F0A3BFF6-F8F9-40E2-8031-2FEFD66FE8F3}" />
    <FieldRef ID="{F6057985-C41D-4A30-8342-FF4E815BA51F}" />
    <FieldRef ID="{4B57EC1E-C6CD-4197-ABEF-81754013DDD4}" />
    <FieldRef ID="{68C1C89A-324D-48C3-AB1E-26AA7003A37F}" />
    <FieldRef ID="{83856973-C1B3-401A-8687-52633D8B2ADC}" />
    <FieldRef ID="{EF890C5F-0DE6-44D6-B994-BC269E830E0E}" />
  </FieldRefs>

</ContentType>
```

17. Next we will identify the attributes of the `ListTemplate` element which completes the configuration for the new List Definition:

```
<ListTemplate
 Name="DelegationDefinition"
 DisallowContentTypes="FALSE"
 Type="12002"
 BaseType="0"
 OnQuickLaunch="FALSE"
 SecurityBits="11"
 Sequence="411"
 DisplayName="Delegation List Definition"
 Description="Delegation List Definition"
 Image="/_layouts/images/itgen.png"/>
</Elements>
```

Defining a custom action group and action

Since this list is primarily for administrative purposes, and not for general site content, it is a good idea to provide a link to the list on the **Site Settings** page. To add a link to any of the standard menus or ribbon, you will need to define a custom action. The groups of links are called action groups, and in order to distinguish this action from the other standard actions, we will also define a custom action group.

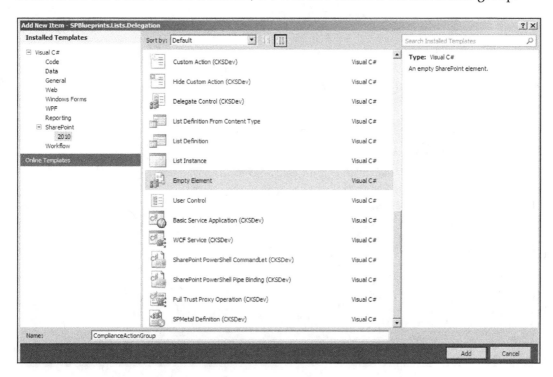

To create the custom action:

1. **Add New Item** to the Visual Studio project.

2. Under the **SharePoint 2010** category, select the **Empty Element** type and provide a name such as ComplianceActionGroup as displayed in the **Add New Item** form in the previous screenshot.

3. Edit the Elements.xml to define the custom action group as follows:

```
<CustomActionGroup Id="e5086212-6073-47e4-9f83-085e3d30d8df"
  Title="Compliance"
  Description="SPBlueprints Compliance Items"
  Location="Microsoft.SharePoint.SiteSettings"
  ImageUrl=
    "/_layouts/images/SPBlueprints/SPBlueprints_Bullet.png"  />
```

With the action group defined, we can now define our custom action as follows:

1. **Add New Item** to the Visual Studio project.

2. Under the **SharePoint 2010** category, select the **Empty Element** type and provide a name such as ViewDelegationLog as displayed in the following screenshot:

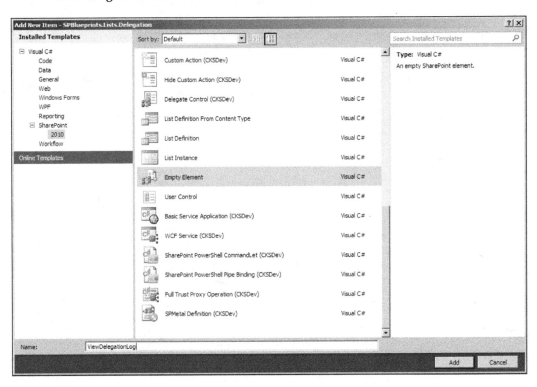

3. Edit the Elements.xml file with the following content to complete the configuration of the CustomAction definition:

```
<CustomAction Description="View Delegation Log"
 GroupId="e5086212-6073-47e4-9f83-085e3d30d8df"
 Id="cdbb5ebd-8599-41d2-8e54-c332d03242c1"
 Location="Microsoft.SharePoint.SiteSettings"
 RegistrationType="ContentType"
 RegistrationId="0x010089E3E6DB8C9B4B3FBB980447E313CE97"
 RequireSiteAdministrator="true"
 Rights="ManageWeb"
 Sequence="12001"
 Title="View Delegation Log">
  <UrlAction Url="Lists/Delegation" />
</CustomAction>
```

Finalizing the delegation list feature

With all of the project items created we can now finalize the **SPBlueprints Delegation List Feature**.

To configure the **SPBlueprints Delegation List Feature**:

1. Rename the **Feature1** item **SPBlueprints Delegation List Feature**.

2. Select the SPBlueprints Delegation List Feature.feature item and provide a **Title** and **Description**. It should resemble the next screenshot.

3. To build the project, select **Build**, then **Build** SPBlueprints.Lists. Delegation.

4. To deploy to the local server, select **Build**, then **Deploy** SPBlueprints. Lists.Delegation.

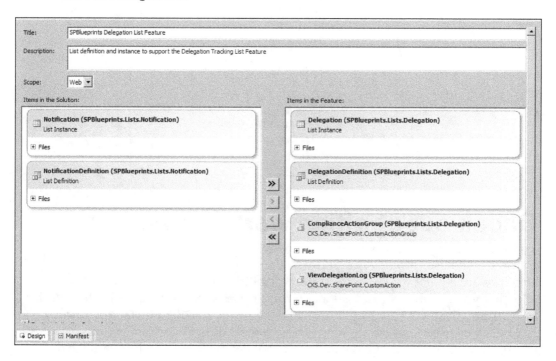

The completed project structure should resemble the following screenshot:

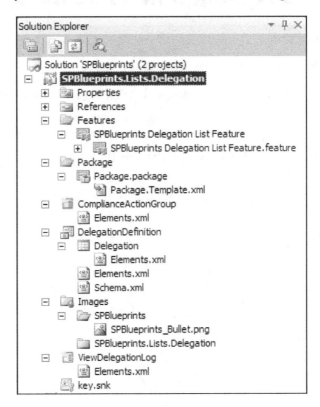

Check out of office workflow activity

To support the workflow we will now create a custom workflow activity that can connect to the user profiles and perform a series of actions. Custom workflow activities are a great way to expand the capabilities of a SharePoint workflow allowing you to connect to additional farm services such as the User Profile Service application, Business Connectivity Services, or even managed metadata services. It can also be used to integrate with other systems directly for cases where Business Connectivity Services is not available or is not desirable. Another advantage to building custom workflow activities is that you can group multiple steps together into one reusable activity.

Approach

The `CheckOutOfOffice` activity will accept a username and perform the following steps:

1. Check the user's profile to see if they are Out of Office, with a delegate specified.

2. If they are:
    - Log the delegation decision in the workflow's history
    - Log the task information to the Master Delegation Tracking List
    - Return delegated username

3. If no match is made, the original username will be returned.

Logging the delegation decision is important and may be required if this is a formal process that could be audited. It will be important to show why the workflow was assigned to the delegate, instead of the primary assignee. Without this, it is likely that there will be questions about what the workflow is doing and the assignment may be looked on as erroneous.

Logging the task information to the Master Delegation Tracking List will provide additional compliance traceability across all of your processes, in addition to providing a source to provide a list of all delegated tasks. This information will be presented as part of the display created in the *View Delegation History page* section.

Creating CheckOutOfOfficeActivity

To start, open Visual Studio 2010 and create an **Empty SharePoint Project** as a farm solution following the same steps outlined for the custom Web Part in *Chapter 1, Building an Effective Intranet*. The project should be called `SPBlueprints.Activities`, and the feature should be renamed `Custom Activities` with a **Title** of `SPBlueprints Custom Activities`.

The next step is to add the required references to the following DLLs:

- `Microsoft.Office.Server`
- `Microsoft.Office.Server.UserProfiles`
- `Microsoft.SharePoint.WorkflowActions`
- `System.Workflow.ComponentModel`

Then add an **Empty Element SPI** to the project called `CheckOutOfOfficeActivity` which will be the name of the workflow activity we are adding.

CheckOutOfOfficeActivity.cs

Now that we have a container for our workflow activity, add in a new class called `CheckOutOfOfficeActivity.cs`.

Edit the `CheckOutOfOfficeActivity.cs` and add the following namespace references:

```
System.Workflow.ComponentModel
Microsoft.SharePoint
Microsoft.SharePoint.Administration
Microsoft.SharePoint.Workflow
Microsoft.SharePoint.WorkflowActions
Microsoft.Office.Server
Microsoft.Office.Server.UserProfiles
```

With the `System.Workflow.ComponentModel` now referenced, change the class definition to:

```
public partial class CheckOutOfOfficeActivity : Activity
```

> Once the override for the `Activity` class has been added you will notice the classes' icon changes to one used for component classes. Double-clicking on the class will now show a designer interface. To view the code right-click and select the **View Code** option.

We now need to define the activity's properties. In order to interact with the workflow, the `__Context` property must be defined in all the workflow activities. The `__Context` property will include contextual information about the workflow calling it, including its status and who initiated it. Next you define any other properties that will be used as parameters. In this case we will define properties for `User`, `AssignTo`, and `Delegated`.

```
public WorkflowContext __Context
{
  get { return (WorkflowContext)GetValue(__ContextProperty); }
  set { SetValue(__ContextProperty, value); }
}

public static readonly DependencyProperty __ContextProperty =
 DependencyProperty.Register("__Context", typeof(WorkflowContext),
 typeof(CheckOutOfOfficeActivity));

public string User
{
```

```
    get { return (string)GetValue(UserProperty); }
    set { SetValue(UserProperty, value); }
}
public static readonly DependencyProperty UserProperty =
 DependencyProperty.Register("User", typeof(string),
 typeof(CheckOutOfOfficeActivity));

public string AssignTo
{
  get { return GetValue(AssignToProperty) as String; }
  set { SetValue(AssignToProperty, value); }
}

public static readonly DependencyProperty AssignToProperty =
 DependencyProperty.Register("AssignTo", typeof(String),
 typeof(CheckOutOfOfficeActivity));

public string Delegated
{
  get { return GetValue(DelegatedProperty) as string; }
  set { SetValue(DelegatedProperty, value); }
}

public static readonly DependencyProperty DelegatedProperty =
 DependencyProperty.Register("Delegated", typeof(string),
 typeof(CheckOutOfOfficeActivity));
```

The main override method for the Activity class is the Execute method which fires when the ActivityExecutionStatus is set to Executing. The work takes place within a using block for the __Context.Site object to ensure proper disposal.

```
protected override ActivityExecutionStatus
Execute(ActivityExecutionContext executionContext)
{
  using (SPSite site = __Context.Site)
  {

      //Read User Profile Code Here

  }

  return ActivityExecutionStatus.Closed;
}
```

Within the activity code we will get the SPServiceContext for the current site, and then use that to establish a connection with the UserProfileManager object, so that we can load the profile for the requested user along with the specific properties defined to support the out of office delegation solution. If the fields do not exist or do not have values, the catch block will be triggered and the initial user will be set as the AssignTo.

```
try
{
  SPServiceContext context = SPServiceContext.GetContext(site);
  UserProfileManager profileManager = new
  UserProfileManager(context);
  UserProfile profile = profileManager.GetUserProfile(this.User);
  DateTime startDate =
  Convert.ToDateTime(profile["outStartDate"].Value);
  DateTime endDate =
  Convert.ToDateTime(profile["outEndDate"].Value);
  string userDelegate = profile["outDelegation"].ToString();

  //Out of Office Check Code Here
}
catch
{
  this.AssignTo = this.User;
  this.Delegated = "False";
}
```

Next is the all-important check to see if the current time falls between the out of office start date and end date and that a delegate has been identified. If a delegate is found, the AssignTo is set to the delegate and the Delegated property is set to "True", otherwise the AssignTo property is set to the original value and the Delegated property is set to "False".

```
if ((System.DateTime.Now >= startDate) && (System.DateTime.Now <=
 endDate) && (userDelegate != ""))
{
//User is out of office with a delegate value, assign delegate
  this.AssignTo = userDelegate;
  this.Delegated = "True";

//Log To Workflow History Code Here

}
else
{
```

```
//User is not out of the office, or a delegate cannot be assigned
  this.AssignTo = this.User;
  this.Delegated = "False";
}
```

Within the delegation block, we will now log the delegation to the workflow history list so that it is clear why the assignment was changed. In order to save the entry we must run with elevated permissions.

```
SPSecurity.RunWithElevatedPrivileges(delegate()
{
string message = string.Format("The task has been delegated from
  {0} to {1}",    this.User.ToString(), this.AssignTo.ToString());

ISharePointService spService =
(ISharePointService)executionContext.GetService(typeof(ISharePoint
Service));
spService.LogToHistoryList(this.WorkflowInstanceId,
  SPWorkflowHistoryEventType.WorkflowComment, -1,
  TimeSpan.MinValue, "Task Delegated", message, String.Empty);
});
//Add Entry to the Master Delegation Log
```

After the item is logged to the workflow's history, we then want to log it to the Master Delegation Log.

One technique I would like to introduce here is using the property bags within the SharePoint objects to store custom configuration data. This provides an alternative to modifying the `web.config` or storing the information in a hidden SharePoint list. In this case we will store our properties at the web-application level. The properties can be viewed and managed using a client tool like SharePoint Manager (`http://spm.codeplex.com/`) or with a server feature such as SharePoint Property Bag Settings 2010 (`http://pbs2010.codeplex.com/`).

For this example, we will read the delegation log's site URL and list GUID from the web application's property bag.

```
string errBlockMessage = "Error reading properties";
try
{
  SPWebApplication webApp = site.WebApplication;
  string logSiteUrl =
   webApp.Properties["_DelegateLogSite"].ToString();
  Guid logGuid = new
   Guid(webApp.Properties["_DelegateLogList"].ToString());
 string ctGuid =
   webApp.Properties["_DelegateContentType"].ToString();
```

To help ensure the process has the ability to write to the Master Delegation Log, we will run the next block of code with elevated privileges. Using elevated privileges will run the code under the identity of the application pool account and will have access to all lists within that web application. Using the information previously loaded from the property bag, we will connect to the web and add a new list item, specifying our field values and then finish by calling the Update method.

```
SPSecurity.RunWithElevatedPrivileges(delegate()
{
  errBlockMessage = "Error connecting to list";
  using (SPWeb logSite = new SPSite(logSiteUrl).RootWeb)
  {
    SPUser userOrig = logSite.EnsureUser(this.User);
    SPUser userDiag = logSite.EnsureUser(this.AssignTo);
    SPList list = logSite.Lists[logGuid];

    errBlockMessage = "Error logging delegation";
    SPListItem logEntry = list.Items.Add();
    logEntry["Title"] = "Delegation Entry";
    logEntry["SiteName"] = __Context.Web.Url.ToString();
    logEntry["ListName"] = __Context.ListId.ToString();
    logEntry["WorkflowName"] =
      __Context.WorkflowInstanceId.ToString();
    logEntry["OrigUser"] = userOrig;
    logEntry["DelegUser"] = userDiag;
    logEntry["LogDate"] = System.DateTime.Now;
    logEntry.Update();
  }
});
}
```

If any error is encountered within the block of code that reads the settings, connects to the list, and adds a list item the issue will be logged to the workflow history list. In addition to logging the actual error message, we are also providing some additional detail to pinpoint where within the block the failure occurred. The three areas include reading the property bag, connecting to the list, and logging the delegation.

In this case we are handling the error instead of raising the error and stopping the process. At this point in the multiple step process we have properly set a valid delegation so there is no good reason to halt the process and prevent it from moving forward. In this case, logging the item to the Master Delegation List, while desirable, is not critical to the success of the individual workflow.

```
catch (Exception ex)
{
  SPSecurity.RunWithElevatedPrivileges(delegate()
  {
    SPDiagnosticsService.Local.WriteTrace(0, new
    SPDiagnosticsCategory("SP Blueprints Workflow Activities",
    TraceSeverity.Unexpected, EventSeverity.Error),
    TraceSeverity.Unexpected, ex.Message, ex.StackTrace);

    string errorMessage = string.Format("{0}: {1}",
     errBlockMessage, ex.Message);

    ISharePointService spService =
  (ISharePointService)executionContext.GetService(typeof(ISharePoint
  Service));
    spService.LogToHistoryList(this.WorkflowInstanceId,
      SPWorkflowHistoryEventType.WorkflowError, -1,
      TimeSpan.MinValue, "Error", errorMessage, String.Empty);
  });
}
```

Next we need to override the `HandleFault` method where we will log any errors that might be generated. Again we will need to run with elevated privileges in order to read the trace information and write out the exception to the workflow's history log.

```
protected override ActivityExecutionStatus
HandleFault(ActivityExecutionContext executionContext, Exception
 ex)
{
  SPSecurity.RunWithElevatedPrivileges(delegate()
  {
    SPDiagnosticsService.Local.WriteTrace(0, new
      SPDiagnosticsCategory("SP Blueprints Workflow Activities",
      TraceSeverity.Unexpected, EventSeverity.Error),
      TraceSeverity.Unexpected, ex.Message, ex.StackTrace);

    string errorMessage = string.Format("Error reading User
      Profile Property: {0}", ex.Message);
```

```
      ISharePointService spService =
      (ISharePointService)executionContext.GetService(typeof(ISharePoint
      Service));
          spService.LogToHistoryList(this.WorkflowInstanceId,
            SPWorkflowHistoryEventType.WorkflowError, -1,
            TimeSpan.MinValue, "Error", errorMessage, String.Empty);
      });

      return base.HandleFault(executionContext, ex);
    }
```

CheckOutOfOfficeActivity elements.xml

The `elements.xml` file for a workflow activity is used to define the
`WorkflowActions` so that it can be interpreted from the design environment.
It describes the action and is used to reference the class and `Assembly` used to
provide the functionality.

The `RuleDesigner` `Sentence` defines the description and field bindings within the
design environment. Then the formal parameters are defined including data type
and direction.

```xml
<?xml version="1.0" encoding="utf-8"?>
<Elements xmlns="http://schemas.microsoft.com/sharepoint/">
  <WorkflowActions>
    <Action Name="Check Out of Office"
    ClassName="SPBlueprints.Activities.CheckOutOfOfficeActivity"
    Assembly="$SharePoint.Project.AssemblyFullName$"
    AppliesTo="all"
    UsesCurrentItem="false"
    Category="SP Blueprints">
      <RuleDesigner Sentence="Check user %1 for Out of Office
        (Assign Task to %2, Delegated? %3)">
       <FieldBind Field="User" Text="User" Id="1"
         DesignerType="TextArea" />
       <FieldBind Field="AssignTo" Text="Assign To" Id="2"
         DesignerType="ParameterNames" />
       <FieldBind Field="Delegated" Text="Delegated" Id="3"
         DesignerType="ParameterNames" />
      </RuleDesigner>
      <Parameters>
       <Parameter Name="__Context"
       Type="Microsoft.SharePoint.WorkflowActions.WorkflowContext"
       Direction="In" />
        <Parameter Name="User" Type="System.String, mscorlib"
          Direction="In" />
        <Parameter Name="AssignTo"  Type="System.String, mscorlib"
```

```
          Direction="Out" />
        <Parameter Name="Delegated"  Type="System.String,
          mscorlib" Direction="Out" />
      </Parameters>
    </Action>
  </WorkflowActions>
</Elements>
```

Adding the web.config authorizedType entry

In order for the custom activity to load, an entry must be added to the authorizedTypes list of web.config. This will identify the assembly as being safe for use. It is possible to automate the entry as part of a feature receiver, but there can be problems managing the entry with multiple activations and deactivations at the site collection level.

The easiest way to manage this is to add the following entry to the <authorizedTypes> group:

```
<authorizedType Assembly="SPBlueprints.Activities,
  Version=1.0.0.0,
  Culture=neutral,
  PublicKeyToken=efa40a16752cda27"
  Namespace="SPBlueprints.Activities"
  TypeName="*"
  Authorized="True" />
```

Completed solution

The completed solution structure is displayed in the following screenshot:

Sample workflow—check out of office

Next we will create a workflow to demonstrate the capabilities of the out of office delegation activity. This activity can be used in any workflow to support a number of different scenarios.

Please note, to create this workflow, the previously built solutions must be deployed and activated. The properties for the Master Delegation Log must also be set for the web application.

To create the workflow, Open SharePoint Designer 2010 and create a new workflow bound to a list on the current site as displayed in the following screenshot:

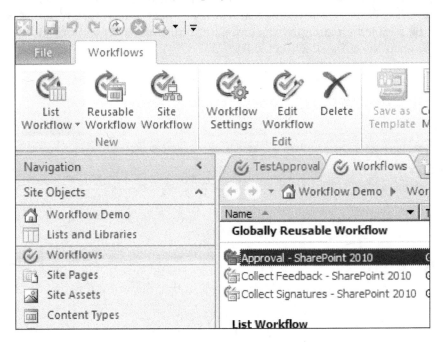

When the workflow editing forms load, the custom action will be loaded and will be available in the list of available actions as shown in the following screenshot:

When added to the workflow it should display as shown in the following screenshot:

Check user <u>User</u> for Out of Office (Assign Task to <u>Variable: Assign To</u> , Delegated? <u>Variable: Delegated</u>)

A sample workflow supporting multiple task levels, each with Out of Office delegation checks, is shown in the following screenshot:

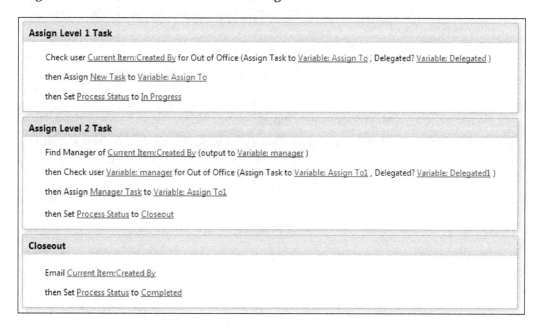

Creating a Task Delegation Web Part

We will now create a custom Web Part for the task delegations to provide better visibility of the current delegation settings, simplify editing the settings, and also to view the delegation history for the given user. This Web Part can be used on the user profile page, or on any of the sites used to store workflows.

In order to determine the correct user profile to read, the Web Part must be able to check the URL for the `accountname` variable, and if not found, use the current user's information, which is how the user profile's `Person.aspx` page operates.

Creating the Web Part project

The Task Delegation Web Part and the referenced application pages will be added to a new project called `SPBlueprints.Delegation`.

To create the initial project:

1. Open Visual Studio 2010.
2. Select **File**, then **New Project**.
3. Browse the **Installed Templates** and select **Visual C# | SharePoint 2010**, and then **Empty SharePoint Project**.
4. Enter the project details such as **Name, Location**, and **Solution name**.
5. Within the **SharePoint Customization Wizard**, provide a path to your SharePoint site and then be sure to select the option to **Deploy as a farm solution**.
6. Right-click on the project file and select **Add** then **New Item**.
7. From the template selection screen select the **Web Part** option.
8. Provide the name `DelegationWebPart` and click on the **Add** button.
9. Rename the **Feature1** item `Web Part`.
10. Select the `Web Part.feature` item and provide a **Title** and a **Description**.

The completed Web Part feature should look like the following screenshot:

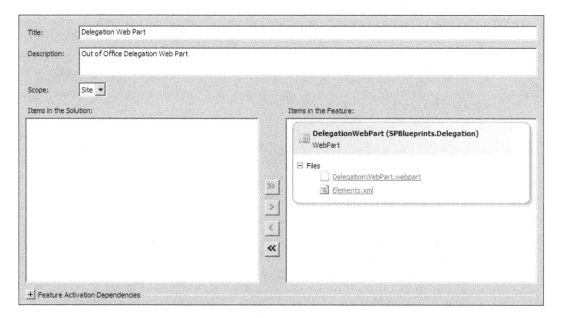

Displaying Out of Office delegation

We will now build the Task Delegation Web Part by editing the
`DelegationWebPart.cs` class file.

First we will define the `getAccountname()` method, which will check the query
string for a variable named `accountname`. If a value is not found, the current user
will be used.

```
private string getAccountname(){
  string queryString =
   System.Web.HttpContext.Current.Request.QueryString.ToString();
  int startPos = queryString.IndexOf("accountname=") + 12;
  int valueLength;
  if (startPos >= 12) {
    int nextPos = queryString.IndexOf("&", startPos);
    if (nextPos > 0){
      valueLength = queryString.IndexOf("&", startPos) - startPos;
    }
    else {
      valueLength = queryString.Length - startPos;
    }
```

```
        return HttpUtility.UrlDecode(queryString.Substring(startPos,
          valueLength));
      }
    if(accountname == "") {
      return
        System.Web.HttpContext.Current.User.Identity.Name.ToString();
      }
    return String.Empty;
    }
```

The `Display` method will be used to render the output for the Web Part. The formatted output will be maintained in the `StringBuilder` object named `output`. We will start by defining the needed variables and reading the current context, so that we can work with the current site's object, and then call the `getAccountname()` method, as previously explained.

```
void Display()
{
  StringBuilder output = new StringBuilder();
  string startDate;
  string endDate;

  SPContext context = SPContext.Current;
  SPSite site = context.Site;

  try{
    accountname = getAccountname();
```

Next we will get the current service context based on the current site and use that to make a connection to the User Profile service, so that the user profile can be read, and the Out of Office delegation properties extracted.

```
SPServiceContext svcContext = SPServiceContext.GetContext(site);
UserProfileManager profileManager = new
 UserProfileManager(svcContext);
UserProfile profile = profileManager.GetUserProfile(accountname);
DateTime dStartDate =
 Convert.ToDateTime(profile["outStartDate"].Value);
startDate = dStartDate.ToShortDateString();

DateTime dEndDate =
 Convert.ToDateTime(profile["outEndDate"].Value);
endDate = dEndDate.ToShortDateString();
```

```
string userDelegate = profile["outDelegation"].ToString();

// Lookup Display name for delegate
profile = profileManager.GetUserProfile(userDelegate);
string userDelegateDisplay = profile.DisplayName.ToString();
string userDelegateProfile = profileManager.MySiteHostUrl +
  "person.aspx";
```

With the supporting data read from the user profiles, we can now format the output. The first step is to reference the Javascript file that is used to launch the Client OM's modal dialog windows. Next we will determine if there is a valid delegation in place, and display the appropriate output.

```
// Reference script
output.AppendFormat(@"<script type='text/ecmascript'
src='/_layouts/SPBlueprints.Delegation/Delegation.js'></script>");

// Determine if Active Delegation
if ((System.DateTime.Now >= dStartDate) && (System.DateTime.Now <=
 dEndDate) && (userDelegate != "")){
  output.AppendFormat(@"<br /><div id='delegationContainer'>Active
    Delegation<br />");
  output.AppendFormat(@"{0} to {1} <br />", startDate, endDate);
  output.AppendFormat(@"Delegating to <a
    href='{0}?accountname={1}'>{2}</a><br /><br />",
    userDelegateProfile, userDelegate, userDelegateDisplay);
  output.AppendFormat(@"<a
    href=""javascript:showDelegationHistory('{0}');"";>View
    Delegation History</a>  -  <a
    href=""javascript:showDelegationForm('{0}');"">Modify
    Delegation Settings</a><br /><br />", accountname.Replace("\\",
    "\\\\"));
  output.AppendFormat(@"</div>");

}
else {outputInactive(output);}
}

catch  // properties could not be loaded
  {   outputInactive(output); }
```

Once the output is complete we will set the value for the literal which renders the output of the Web Part.

```
this.EnsureChildControls();
this.literalMessage.Text = output.ToString();
```

Since the output for the inactive delegation could be called from more than one place, the code to display that version was moved to the outputInactive() method which is called in the previous code.

```
private StringBuilder outputInactive(StringBuilder output){
// Output Inactive Delegation
  output.AppendFormat(@"<div id='delegationContainer'>No Active
  Delegation<br />");
  output.AppendFormat(@"<br /><br />");
  output.AppendFormat(@"<br /><br />");
  output.AppendFormat(@"<a
  href='javascript:showDelegationHistory({0});');>View Delegation
  History</a>  -  <a
  href='javascript:showDelegationForm({0});'>Modify Delegation
  Settings</a>", accountname.Replace("\\",  "\\\\"));
  output.AppendFormat(@"</div>");
  return output;
}
```

Delegation.js

When using Javascript within your custom Web Parts, it is often easiest to add the content to a file that is managed with the custom Web Part's feature. By mapping the Layouts folder in your Visual Studio project, it is possible to deploy files to a location within the Layouts virtual directory making it available to any site in the farm.

Best practice is to name the folder to match your project or feature name. In this case a folder named SPBlueprints.Delegation has been added and the following Delegation.js script was added to the project:

```
function showDelegationHistory(account) {
  var _options = { url:
    '/_layouts/SPBlueprints.Delegation/ViewDelegationHistory.aspx?
    accountname=' + account, width: '800', title: 'Delegation
    History for ' + account };
  SP.UI.ModalDialog.showModalDialog(_options);
}
```

```
function showDelegationForm(account) {
  var _options = { url:
  '/_layouts/SPBlueprints.Delegation/EditDelegationSettings.aspx?
  accountname=' + account, width: '800', title: 'Edit Delegaton
  Settings'};
  SP.UI.ModalDialog.showModalDialog(_options);
}
```

Displaying the Task Delegation Web Part

The rendered Task Delegation Web Part is displayed in the following screenshot:

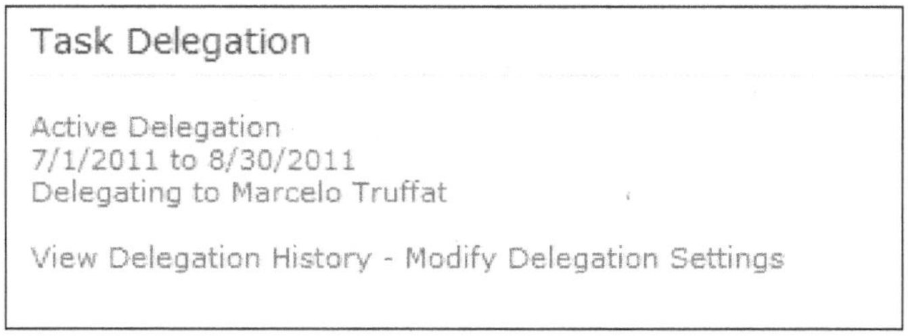

```
Task Delegation

Active Delegation
7/1/2011 to 8/30/2011
Delegating to Marcelo Truffat

View Delegation History - Modify Delegation Settings
```

Creating custom application pages

The Task Delegation Web Part includes references to two separate application pages. Custom application pages are ASP.NET pages that can fully utilize the server API, and ASP.NET capabilities to deliver robust visualizations, or a web form with complex business rules. The application pages are deployed to the Layouts directory that are available throughout the system.

Preparing for custom application pages

In order to add application pages or any other object to the Layouts directory, we start by mapping the path to the directory. Since these application pages will be a dependency for the Task Delegation Web Part, we will add these pages to the existing project. To do this, right-click on the project name and select **Add**, then **SharePoint "Layouts" Mapped Folder**. This will create a new folder called Layouts in your project.

View Delegation History page

Logging the delegations is important to keep a central tracking list, but we will also want to provide an easy way to view the delegation data. In the Task Delegation Web Part we added a link that references the View Delegation History page where we can show the delegation history for the specified user. Putting this in an application page will make it available throughout the farm. The Master Delegation Lists' properties can be read from the web application's property bag, giving you the ability to use the single page throughout the farm, even if there are multiple delegation lists.

The page will read the `accountname` variable provided in the query string, connect to the web application's Master Delegation List, and display the output in a standard ASP.NET datagrid.

This page could easily be extended to include some advanced filtering capabilities, perhaps based on specific date ranges, or based on who it was delegated to.

To add the custom application page:

1. Expand the `Layouts` directory mapped in the previous section.

2. Select the `SPBlueprints.Delegation` folder.

3. Right-click and select **Add**, then **New Item**.

4. Under the **SharePoint 2010** category, select **Application Page** and provide the name `ViewDelegationHistory.aspx` as displayed in the following screenshot:

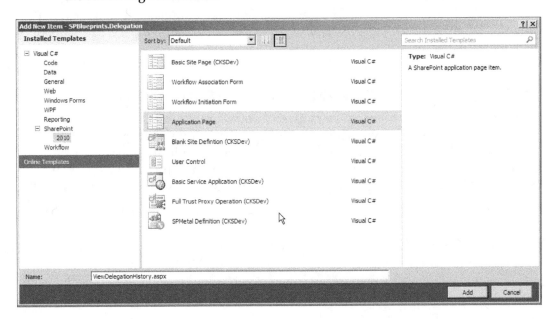

ViewDelegationHistory.aspx

As application pages are ASP.NET pages, they contain both the design interface for controls and the code behind for logic and events.

Within the `ViewDelegationHistory.aspx` page, the normal display content should be added to the `PlaceHolderMain` content control. Any filtering controls or additional content should be added to this section. For now, we will include a label for displaying any rendering errors and the single `GridView` control for displaying the delegation history information.

```
<asp:Content ID="Main"
  ContentPlaceHolderID="PlaceHolderMain"
  runat="server">
    <asp:Label ID="Error"
      runat="server"></asp:Label><br />
    <asp:GridView ID="delegationHistory"
      runat="server"
      BorderWidth="0"
      CssClass="ms-listviewtable">
    </asp:GridView>
</asp:Content>
```

A title should also be added to the `PageTitle` and `PageTitleInTitleArea` content areas as follows:

```
<asp:Content ID="PageTitle"
  ContentPlaceHolderID="PlaceHolderPageTitle"
  runat="server">
  View Delegation History
</asp:Content>

<asp:Content ID="PageTitleInTitleArea"
  ContentPlaceHolderID="PlaceHolderPageTitleInTitleArea"
  runat="server" >
  View Delegation History
</asp:Content>
```

ViewDelegationHistory.aspx.cs

The `ViewDelegationHistory.aspx.cs` is a regular ASP.NET code behind page, with all of the available page lifecycle events and capabilities.

Since we will be working with the user profiles, as well as the web application's property bag, we will need to add the following references to our class:

```
using Microsoft.SharePoint.Administration;
using Microsoft.SharePoint.WebControls;
using Microsoft.Office.Server;
using Microsoft.Office.Server.UserProfiles;
```

We will also define the string `accountname` for use throughout the methods on the page.

```
private string accountname;
```

To get started we will need to know what account name was provided in the query string. A call to the `getAccountname()` method will set the `accountname` variable.

```
private void getAccountname()
{
  string queryString =
   System.Web.HttpContext.Current.Request.QueryString.ToString();
  int startPos = queryString.IndexOf("accountname=") + 12;
  int valueLength;

  if (startPos >= 12) {
    int nextVariable = queryString.IndexOf("&", startPos);
    if (nextVariable > 0){
      valueLength = queryString.IndexOf("&", startPos) - startPos;
    }
    else{
      valueLength = queryString.Length - startPos;
    }
    accountname= Server.UrlDecode(queryString.Substring(startPos,
     valueLength));
  }
}
```

The data is loaded through a method named `loadDelegationHistory()` which reads the delegation list's location from the web application's property bag.

```
private DataTable loadDelegationHistory()
{
  Try{
    SPContext context = SPContext.Current;
    SPSite site = context.Site;
    SPWebApplication webApp = site.WebApplication;
    string logSiteUrl =
```

```
       webApp.Properties["_DelegateLogSite"].ToString();
   Guid logGuid = new
       Guid(webApp.Properties["_DelegateLogList"].ToString());
```

Next we will connect to the web where the list is located and load the list:

```
using (SPSite tmpSite = new SPSite(logSiteUrl)){
    SPWeb logSite = tmpSite.RootWeb;
    SPUser userOrig = logSite.EnsureUser(accountname);
    SPList history = logSite.Lists[logGuid];
```

In order to only get the fields and records we are looking for, we will now format a query using the SPQuery object.

```
       SPQuery query = new SPQuery();
       query.ViewFields = @"<FieldRef Name='ID' /><FieldRef
       Name='SiteName' /><FieldRef Name='ListName' /><FieldRef
       Name='WorkflowName' /><FieldRef Name='LogDate' /><FieldRef
       Name='OrigUser' /><FieldRef Name='DelegUser' />";
       query.Query = @"<Where><Eq><FieldRef Name='OrigUser'
        /><Value Type='User'>" + userOrig.Name.ToString() +
        "</Value></Eq></Where>";
```

With the objects loaded and the query formatted, we can now return the DataTable object with the list data returned.

```
       return history.GetItems(query) GetDataTable();
   }
}
```

In order to handle errors and still return a DataTable object, we will create a DataTable object and populate it with any exceptions that may be generated as part of the catch block.

```
catch (Exception ex) {
   DataTable tableHistory = new DataTable();
   tableHistory.Columns.Add("Error");
   DataRow errorRow = tableHistory.NewRow();
   errorRow.SetField("Error", ex.Message);
   tableHistory.Rows.Add(errorRow);

   return tableHistory;
  }
}
```

With the supporting methods defined, we can now define the main controlling code within the `Page_Load()` method which is the standard starting point for the ASP. NET pages. We will include some error handling and only execute the page if it is not loaded in a postback event.

```
protected void Page_Load(object sender, EventArgs e)
{
  try
  {
    this.Error.Text = "";
    this.Error.Visible = false;

    if (!Page.IsPostBack){
```

The `getAccountname()` and `loadDelegationHistory()` methods are now called to get the `accountname` property and then load the list data.

```
        getAccountname();
        DataTable userHistory = loadDelegationHistory();
```

Since the `Modified` and `Created` fields are returned by default, we will remove these tables from the list data returned before the datagrid is bound to the returned `DataTable`.

```
        if (userHistory.Columns[0].ColumnName != "Error"){
                //Exclude these columns
          userHistory.Columns.Remove("Modified");
          userHistory.Columns.Remove("Created");
        }
        this.delegationHistory.BorderStyle =
         System.Web.UI.WebControls.BorderStyle.None;
        this.delegationHistory.Width =
         System.Web.UI.WebControls.Unit.Percentage(100);
        this.delegationHistory.DataSource = userHistory;
        this.delegationHistory.DataBind();
      }
```

The main `catch` block will display any exceptions that occur during the rendering of the content and then closes out the `Page_Load()` method.

```
    }
    catch (Exception ex){
      this.Error.Visible = true;
      this.Error.Text = "Error:  " + ex.Message;
    }
  }
```

Displaying the View Delegation History page

Clicking the View Delegation History link from within the Task Delegation Web Part will display the delegation history as shown in the following screenshot:

Completed SPBlueprints.Delegation solution

The completed solution for the SPBlueprints.Delegation project and Web Part feature should include the delegation Web Part, Delegation.js script file, EditDelegationSettings.aspx application page, and ViewDelegationHistory.aspx application page. The final solution should look like the following screenshot:

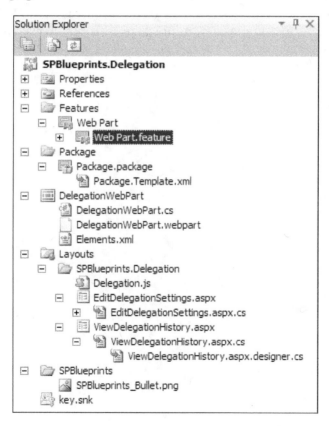

Summary

This section leveraged both the Server and Client OMs to create packaged solutions in order to deliver the Out of Office delegation solution. The customizations are grouped as follows:

- Visual Studio 2010:
    ◦ List Definition
    ◦ List Instance
    ◦ Web Part
    ◦ Action group definition
    ◦ Actions definition
    ◦ Application page

These solutions provide examples of how to extend the user profiles and create customizations that can be used to support business processes, and also how to add additional Web Parts to the user profile page. This can be used as the basis to support robust reusable business processes, and also be used to enhance the value of the user profile pages.

3
Building an Enterprise Content Management Solution

One of SharePoint's core capabilities is to store document-based content. In many cases for informal team scoped documents, but organizations also typically have more formal enterprise content that is stored centrally and relevant to multiple groups. The Document Center template included in SharePoint 2010 offers a good starting point, but unfortunately it cannot scale to the size needed to support medium to large organizations.

The limitations are based on the overall amount of content; stored in a library, site collection, and underlying content database. At the time of writing, Microsoft introduced new guidance with the release of SharePoint 2010 Service Pack 1 which states that the maximum content database size can be 4 TB with SQL and storage sub-system optimization, or 200 GB without optimization.

 Additional details about SharePoint boundaries can be found in the TechNet article *SharePoint Server 2010 capacity management: Software boundaries and limits* available at: `http://technet.microsoft.com/en-us/library/cc262787.aspx`

While it is possible to live within the actual hard limits, performance problems and general usability issues will be noticed well before those limits are reached. Therefore a proper solution should be architected to ensure long term health and viability of the solution, and handle the underlying storage and organization of the document content, along with an easy to use system to find and retrieve this content.

This chapter will take us through some of the initial organization and storage decisions and provide solutions for making the processes of adding and locating content very easy for the users. The covered solutions include:

- Configuring content types for publishing
- Document routing via the Content Organizer
- DocVault Web Part
- Enhanced Document ID redirect Web Part

The following screenshot shows the Document Vault main site:

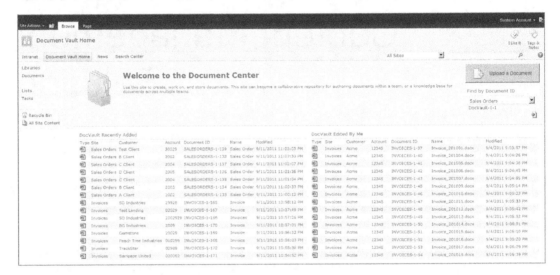

Defining content containers

When planning for content containers, it is important to have a general idea of how much content the system will eventually need to hold. In this sample we will plan for containers to hold invoices, sales orders, and purchase orders.

For the sample system, we expect to store the following documents for up to seven years. The following table shows projections for the number of documents by type per week, per year, as well as the maximum number expected to be stored before retention policies archive the older documents:

Document type	Number per week	Number per year	Expected limit
Invoices	200	10,400	72,800
Sales orders	300	15,600	109,200
Purchase orders	150	7,800	54,600

As we see, the numbers start to grow quickly. If each document averaged 150K in PDF format, the total storage within a single site collection would be difficult to support. Most organizations have close to 15 enterprise document types that they manage, making this planning process even more important.

In addition to the storage needs of the documents, there are also the general organization boundaries of SharePoint to consider including the number of items in a library, folder, or view. In extreme cases, a single document type may need to be stored in multiple document libraries or perhaps within multiple site collections.

To counter these problems the **Enterprise Content Management** (ECM) solution will be organized into the following containers, each a site collection:

Site name	Site template	Notes
Document Vault home	Document Center	Entry site into the ECM solution
Invoices	Document Center	Used to store invoices
Sales orders	Document Center	Used to store sales orders
Purchase orders	Document Center	Used to store purchase orders

Any additional types of documents would be stored in similarly configured site collections.

Any site collections that are expected to be very large should be created in their own content database. That is out of the scope of this book, but can be done with the PowerShell commands `New-SPContentDatabase` followed by `New-SPSite` referencing the previously created content database.

Defining and managing content types

The first step in making the content easy to organize and discover is to define content types and site columns that describe the documents. Classifying content based on a content type makes it easier to locate them later using either list or search based queries.

Content type synchronization

While content types and site columns have traditionally been bound to a single site collection, the 2010 release of SharePoint Sever added a feature called the **content type hub**, which is part of the managed metadata service. This allows you to define all of your content types in a central location, and then to publish specified content types out to other site collections. This is very important for solutions like the one we are creating here as it is likely that content will be stored in multiple site collections.

If your content type hub has not already been defined, then it is important to know that you can only define a single content type hub per managed metadata service application. Proper planning should be done before specifying the site that will serve as the content type hub for all sites and content types.

To set up a content type for publishing:

1. Navigate to the content type.
2. Click on the **Manage publishing for this content type** link.
3. With the **Publish** option selected, click on the **OK** button.

The publishing process is executed via timer jobs and may take a little while to complete. It is possible to execute the jobs immediately, by navigating to the timer job and clicking on the **Run Now** button.

Content type definition

The following content types will be defined for this sample solution. They will be defined in the content type hub site so that they are available for all other site collections.

The DocVault Core content type inherits from the Document content type and includes the following site columns:

Field	Description
Title	Inherited from Document
Customer	Single line of text
Account	Single line of text

The invoices content type inherits from the DocVault Core content type and includes the following site columns:

Field	Description
Title	Inherited from DocVault Core
Customer	Inherited from DocValue Core
Account	Inherited from DocVault Core
Amount	Currency

The sales orders content type inherits from the DocVault Core content type and includes the following site columns:

Field	Description
Title	Inherited from DocVault Core
Customer	Inherited from DocValue Core
Account	Inherited from DocVault Core
Amount	Currency

The purchase orders content type inherits from the DocVault Core content type and includes the following site columns:

Field	Description
Title	Inherited from DocVault Core
Customer	Inherited from DocValue Core
Account	Inherited from DocVault Core
Amount	Currency

After the content types are configured and available on their respective sites, they should be configured as the default content type for the respective libraries.

Document routing

For this solution to be effective and easy for the end users, the process of adding and storing content needs to be simplified. One of the usability hurdles that can make ECM difficult in SharePoint is determining the proper location for your uploaded content. There are also fundamental organization techniques that need to be followed for the system to continue to perform well with large sets of content, mainly limiting the number of documents per folder. These are details that the end user should not have to think about, let alone understand. To handle this, we need an easy way to route documents to the appropriate location. Fortunately, SharePoint 2010 introduced the Content Organizer feature which supports rules-based document organization, including the ability to move documents across site collections. This is a great example of a task that used to require custom code, but can now be configured with out of the box features.

To support this part of the solution we will need to activate the Content Organizer feature on each of the site collections. This will create a document library called Drop Off folder in each of the sites.

To activate the Content Organizer feature:

1. Navigate to the site.
2. Click on the **Site Actions** menu and select **Site Settings**.
3. Under **Site Actions**, click on the **Manage site features** link.
4. Click on the **Activate** button on the Content Organizer line if not already activated.

We can now configure the destination content locations which can be used as part of the Content Organizer feature.

To configure the Content Organizer destinations:

1. Navigate to the **Central Administration** site.
2. Under the **General Application Settings** heading, click on the **Configure Send to connections** link.
3. Ensure that the **New Connection** option is selected.
4. Provide a **Display name**.

5. Provide a **Send To** URL, which would be the path to the site collection with Content Organizer turned on with `/_vti_bin/officialfile.asmx` added to the end. An example would be `http://intranet/docvault/invoices/_vti_bin/officialfile.asmx`

 If the Content Organizer is not activated, the URL will not validate as a valid location.

6. Set the **Send To Action to Move** in order to prevent a copy from being left in the source library.

7. Provide an explanation if desired.

8. Click on the **Add Connection** button.

9. Repeat for all destinations that need to be configured.

10. Click on the **OK** button.

With the Content Organizer feature activated on each of the sites and the destinations configured, we can now set up the routing rules.

To configure the Content Organizer rules from the DocVault site collection:

1. Navigate to the site.

2. Click on the **Site Actions** menu and select **Site Settings**.

3. Click on the **Content Organizer Settings** link under the **Site Administration** heading.

4. Click on the checkbox labeled **Require users to use the organizer when submitting new content to libraries with one or more organizer rules pointing to them**.

5. Click on the checkbox labeled **Allow rules to specify another site as a target location**.

6. Click on the **OK** button.

7. Click on the **Content Organizer Rules link** under the **Site Administration** heading.

8. Click on the **Add new item** option.

9. Provide a name for the rule; I recommend setting it to the content type.

10. Select the **Content Type Group** and **Type**.

11. Under the **Target Location** section, select the option **Another content organizer in a different site**.

12. Select the desired **Send To** location.

13. Click on the **OK** button.

14. Repeat as needed for each of the content types that need to be routed.

This process will now route any uploaded documents from the DocVault Home site to the Drop Off library of appropriate content type specific site collection. We now need to configure the routing rules to move it from the Drop Off library to its final location in a folder inside a regular document library.

To configure the content type level site collection Content Organizer rules:

1. Navigate to the site.

2. Click on the **Site Actions** menu and select **Site Settings**.

3. Click on the **Content Organizer Settings** link under the **Site Administration** heading.

4. Click on the checkbox labeled **Require users to use the organizer when submitting new content to libraries with one or more organizer rules pointing to them**.

5. Click on the checkbox labeled **Create subfolders after a target location has too many items**.

6. Click on the **OK** button.

7. Click on the **Content Organizer Rules** link under the **Site Administration** heading.

8. Click on the **Add new item** option.

9. Provide a name for the rule, I recommend setting it to the content type.

10. Select the **Content Type Group** and **Type**.

11. Browse to the desired document library.

12. Click on the **OK** button.

With the rules configured on the DocVault Home site collection and the content type specific site collections we now have a robust routing system that can file away the documents in an efficient and effective way. An example of the resulting process flow is shown as follows:

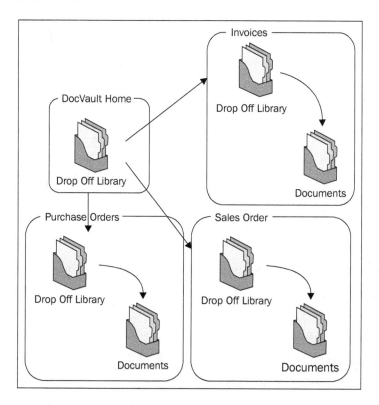

Optimizing Search

Both the regular SharePoint Server Search service application and FAST Search service application offer a rich platform to developers to create dynamic systems that are able to accommodate extremely large datasets. It can be leveraged to provide a way to aggregate content across multiple site collections as we will see in the next section.

The search system is complex, and indeed there are entire books written on the subject, but there are three key pieces that need to be understood as they will be leveraged in this solution:

- Content sources
- Search scopes
- Managed properties

Content sources

Content sources define the locations that will be crawled. This can include both SharePoint resources as well as other systems like Exchange, network shares, or even public websites. Most administrators configure a single content source for SharePoint, and list out the root of each web application. This works fine, but by creating multiple content sources, you can leverage them within the custom search scopes covered in the next sub-section, to filter down the content much more easily. Items from each of the content sources are combined into the singular, all-encompassing index that services the service application.

To configure a custom content source for the DocVault solution:

1. Navigate to the **Search Service Application**.
2. Click on the **Content Sources** link on the Quick Launch menu under the **Crawling** heading.
3. Click on the **New Content Source** menu item.
4. Provide a name such as `DocVault`.
5. As we want this custom content source to include content from each of the DocVault sites, we will add in the path to each of the site collections on a separate line.
6. Under the **Crawl Settings** section select the **Only crawl the Site Collection of each start address** option.
7. You can then schedule an appropriate crawl schedule and save the new scope.

The following screenshot shows an example of the DocVault content source:

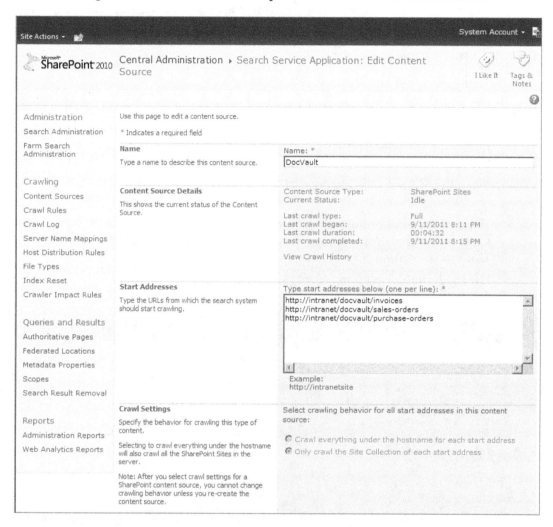

Search scopes

Search scopes are used to filter down the all-encompassing index into subsets of data based on rules. These rules can be set based on where the content is located, the content source that was used to index it, or based on a property of the data.

The two search scopes that come with the system by default are:

- **All Sites**: This scope will search against all content, with no rules applied
- **People**: This search scope filters down to only show the SPSPeople objects, separating out normal content from the user profiles

To support the DocVault system, we are going to configure a custom search scope to be used on the various DocVault sites which will ensure that any results returned are from the DocVault sites.

To create a custom search scope:

1. Navigate to the **Search Service Application**.

2. Click on the **Search Scopes** link on the Quick Launch menu under the **Queries and Results** heading.

3. Provide a **Title** such as DocVault and a **Description**, then click on the **OK** button.

4. From the **View Scopes** page, click on the **Add Rules** link next to the new search scope.

5. To filter the dataset down to just the DocVault sites, we will select the **Content Source** option under the **Scope Rule Type** section and select the **DocVault Content Source** previously defined.

6. For the **Behavior** section, select the **Require** option as shown in the following screenshot:

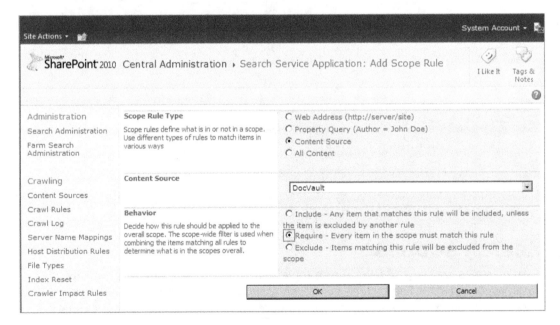

7. From the **Scope Properties** page, select the **New Rule** link.

8. For the **Scope Rule Type** section, select the **Property Query** option.

9. For the **Property Query** section, select the **contentclass** option which will look for specific types of objects within the index.

10. For the property value, add STS_listitem_documentlibrary which will filter the results down to just Document Library list items.

11. For the **Behavior** section, select the **Require** option as shown in the following screenshot:

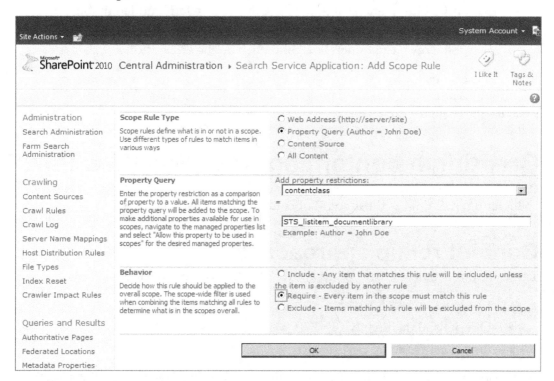

Managed properties

Managed properties provide a way to identify an item based on a specific property or attribute. That is how a site column or list column is indexed and available during the search processing, and can be used for either filtering the results or for display purposes.

To support the DocVault system, we will configure managed properties to support both the Customer and Account (CustomerAccount) fields included in the DocVault Core content type.

To identify a managed property:

1. Navigate to the **Search Service Application**.
2. Click the **Metadata Properties** link under the **Queries and Results** heading.
3. Provide a **Property name** value such as `Customer` and a **Description**.
4. Under the **Mappings to crawled properties** section, click on the **Add Mapping** button and search for the Customer field identified in the content type.
5. Select the **ows_Customer(Text)** and click on the **OK** button.

Repeat these steps for the Account field, but provide the name `CustomerAccount` since there is already a managed property named Account that refers to a person's username.

Creating a content aggregation Web Part

Providing an easy way to access the content is incredibly important, and gets more challenging over time as the amount of content in the system grows.

Content rollup approaches

There are three main content rollup approaches that can be considered:

- Content Query Web Part
- Query list data directly
- Query using SharePoint Search

In the Document Center template, there are three **Content Query Web Parts (CQWP)** that are pre-configured. The CQWP can work great in smaller sites, but has two real limitations; it cannot work across site collections and it does not perform well with very large sets of content. So even if this solution were altered to locate all of the sites and libraries within a single site collection, it is very likely that the solution would fail eventually. Performance is even more critical because those content rollups are typically placed on the main landing pages that all users will see as they enter the system.

A second option is to query all of the sources directly. Those sources could be the specific libraries using the `SPList.GetItems()` method or the `SPWeb.GetSiteData()` method which can be run for each site or site collection that holds the content. Querying the sources directly would require that you know where the content is and will require maintenance to ensure that any new content sources are included in the rollup. In addition, because the source systems are being queried directly, the same performance problems reviewed in the CQWP previously would be experienced here as well.

The third, and preferred option, would be to use the SharePoint Search sub-system to access the content. Getting this information should be substantially quicker because the index has pre-processed the information, and the actual sources do not have to be scanned or queried. With proper planning of the content containers and search, as covered in the previous sections, it is possible to have the content rollups automatically find any applicable new content sources that are added to the system over time to the given search scope. The only downside to using Search is that the content has to be in the index to be discovered and crawls should be scheduled on a regular schedule.

DocVault Listings Web Part

We will now create a custom Web Part that can provide dynamic content rollups across the different DocVault site collections. There are two views available in the initial Web Part, but additional ones can be identified as needed by extending the code and defined `QueryMode` property.

Creating the Web Part

The DocVault Listings Web Part will be added to the previously created `SPBlueprints.WebParts` project created in *Chapter 2, Building an Out of Office Delegation Solution.*

To add the additional Web Part:

1. Open the `SPBlueprints.WebParts` project in Visual Studio 2010.
2. Browse to the **Installed Templates** and select **Visual C# | SharePoint | 2010**.
3. Right-click on the project file and select **Add** then **New Item**.
4. From the template selection screen select the **Web Part** option.
5. Provide the name `DocVaultListings` and click on the **Add** button.

6. Edit the `DocVaultListings.webpart` file with the following definition:

```
<properties>
  <Property Name="Group" type="string">SPBlueprints</Property>
  <property name="Title" type="string">DocVault
    Listings</property>
  <property name="Description" type="string">SPBlueprints - The
    DocVault Rollup web part displays content rollups for
    DocVault documents.</property>
  <property name="SearchProxyName" type="string">Search Service
    Application</property>
  <property name="SearchScopeName"
    type="string">DocVault</property>
  <property name="DisplayLimit" type="int">15</property>
</properties>
```

Importing the needed Web Part and search references

Start by editing the `DocVaultListings.cs` file and add in the following references:

```
using System.Collections;
using System.Data;
using System.Text;
using Microsoft.SharePoint.Administration;
using Microsoft.Office.Server.Search;
using Microsoft.Office.Server.Search.Query;
using Microsoft.Office.Server.Search.Administration;
```

Defining the Web Part properties

Next we will need to define the Web Part's properties starting with the Search Proxy Name property. This property will be used to manage the connection to the Search service application.

```
private string searchProxyName;

[WebBrowsable(true),
 Category("Custom Properties"),
 WebDisplayName("Search Proxy Name"),
 WebDescription("Please provide the name of your Search Service
   Application."),
 Personalizable(PersonalizationScope.Shared)]
public string SearchProxyName
```

```
{
  get { return searchProxyName; }
  set { searchProxyName = value; }
}
```

Next we will define the Search Scope Name property which can be used to target the desirable content for display.

```
private string searchScopeName;
[WebBrowsable(true),
 Category("Custom Properties"),
 WebDisplayName("Search Proxy Name"),
 WebDescription("Please provide the name of your Search Service
  Application."),
 Personalizable(PersonalizationScope.Shared)]
public string SearchProxyName
{
  get { return searchProxyName; }
  set { searchProxyName = value; }
}
```

Next we will define the Display Limit property used to determine how many records to display.

```
private int displayLimit;
[WebBrowsable(true),
 Category("Custom Properties"),
 WebDisplayName("Result limit"),
 WebDescription("The number of items to display."),
 Personalizable(PersonalizationScope.Shared)]
public int DisplayLimit
{
  get { return displayLimit; }
  set { displayLimit = value; }
}
```

In order to provide multiple views, we will add an enum property that will display as a drop-down list from within the Web Part properties page. This requires that we define and set a value so that it can be used within the Web Part.

```
private queryMode _queryMode;
public enum queryMode
{
  ByUser,
  Recent
}
```

```
[WebBrowsable(true),
 Category("Custom Properties"),
 WebDisplayName("Query Mode"),
 WebDescription("Please select the query mode."),
 Personalizable(PersonalizationScope.Shared)]
public queryMode QueryMode
{
  get { return _queryMode; }
  set { _queryMode = value; }
}

public DocVaultListings()
{
  _queryMode = queryMode.ByUser;
}
```

Formatting the Web Part

The output will be built within a literal control defined within the class, and instantiated within the CreateChildControls() method shown as follows:

```
protected Literal _output;
protected override void CreateChildControls()
{
  this._output = new Literal();
  this._output.ID = "output";
  this.Controls.Add(this._output);
}
```

With all of the setup work complete, we can now define the Display() method that can be called from the OnLoad() method. The method starts by defining the StringBuilder class, which we will use to build the output of the Web Part, and then attempts to connect to the Search Proxy specified in the Web Part properties.

```
protected void Display()
{
StringBuilder messages = new StringBuilder();
try
{
SearchQueryAndSiteSettingsServiceProxy settingsProxy =
SPFarm.Local.ServiceProxies.GetValue<SearchQueryAndSiteSettingsSer
viceProxy>();
SearchServiceApplicationProxy searchProxy =
settingsProxy.ApplicationProxies.GetValue<SearchServiceApplication
Proxy>(this.searchProxyName);
FullTextSqlQuery mQuery = new FullTextSqlQuery(searchProxy);
```

Next we will do some preparation work that is common to each of the views.

```
try
{
ResultTableCollection resultsTableCollection;
DataTable results = new DataTable();
bool bAltRow = true;
```

The multiple views of the Web Part are handled by a central switch statement that will check the _queryMode value and display the appropriate view.

```
switch (_queryMode){
  case queryMode.ByUser:

    break;
  case queryMode.Recent:

    break;
}
```

Within the ByUser view, we will construct and execute a query and then format the returned results. The FullTextSQLQuery will grab the desired properties from the specified search scope and filter them based on content generated by the current user. The Display Limit Web Part property will be used to limit the number of results returned. The included output will present the returned data similar to a normal list view, though the complex view functions have not been included.

```
string user = SPContext.Current.Web.CurrentUser.Name;
mQuery.QueryText = "SELECT Title, Customer, CustomerAccount,
LastModifiedTime, DocID, SiteTitle, ContentTypeSearch, CreatedBy,
Filename, FileExtension, Path FROM SCOPE() WHERE (\"scope\" = '" +
searchScopeName + "') AND Author = '" + user + "' ORDER BY
LastModifiedTime Desc";

mQuery.ResultTypes = ResultType.RelevantResults;
mQuery.TrimDuplicates = false;
mQuery.RowLimit = DisplayLimit;
resultsTableCollection = mQuery.Execute();
if (resultsTableCollection.Count > 0)
{
  ResultTable relevantResults =
    resultsTableCollection[ResultType.RelevantResults];
    results.Load(relevantResults, LoadOption.OverwriteChanges);
```

```
messages.AppendFormat(@"<table width='100%' border='0'
  cellpadding='1' cellspacing='0' class='ms-listviewtable'>
  <tr class='ms-viewheadertr ms-vhltr'>
  <td>Type</td><td>Site</td><td>Customer</td>
  <td>Account</td><td>DocumentID</td>
  <td>Name</td><td>Modified</td></tr>");

foreach (DataRow row in results.Rows)
{
  messages.AppendFormat(@"<tr ");
  if (bAltRow) {
    messages.AppendFormat(@"class='ms-alternatingstrong'"); }
    messages.AppendFormat(@"><td><a href='{6}'><img src='{7}'
      border='0'></a></td><td>{0}</td><td>{1}</td><td>{2}</td>
      <td>{3}</td><td><a href='{6}'>{4}</a></td><td>{5}</td></tr>",
      row[5].ToString(), row[1].ToString(), row[2].ToString(),
      row[4].ToString(), row[0].ToString(), row[3].ToString(),
      row[10].ToString(), getImageRef(row[9].ToString()));
    bAltRow = !bAltRow;
  }
  messages.AppendFormat(@"</table>");
}
```

Within the `Recent` view, we will construct and execute a similar query as the `ByUser`, but this query will look for documents recently edited by any user. It will also search against the specified search scope and limit the results to the Display Limit specified in the Web Part property.

```
mQuery.QueryText = "SELECT Title, Customer, CustomerAccount,
LastModifiedTime, DocID, SiteTitle, ContentTypeSearch, CreatedBy,
Filename, FileExtension, Path FROM SCOPE() WHERE (\"scope\" = '" +
searchScopeName + "') AND LastModifiedTime >= DATEADD (DAY, -30,
GETGMTDATE()) ORDER BY LastModifiedTime Desc";

mQuery.ResultTypes = ResultType.RelevantResults;
mQuery.TrimDuplicates = false;
mQuery.RowLimit = DisplayLimit;
resultsTableCollection = mQuery.Execute();
if (resultsTableCollection.Count > 0)
{
  ResultTable relevantResults =
   resultsTableCollection[ResultType.RelevantResults];
  results.Load(relevantResults, LoadOption.OverwriteChanges);
  messages.AppendFormat(@"<table width='100%' border='0'
   cellpadding='1' cellspacing='0' class='ms-listviewtable'>
```

```
    <tr class='ms-viewheadertr msvhltr'>
    <td>Type</td><td>Site</td><td>Customer</td><td>Account</td>
    <td>Document ID</td><td>Name</td><td>Modified</td></tr>");

foreach (DataRow row in results.Rows)
{
  messages.AppendFormat(@"<tr ");
  if (bAltRow) {
    messages.AppendFormat(@"class='ms-alternatingstrong'"); }
    messages.AppendFormat(@"><td><a href='{6}'><img src='{7}'
    border='0'></a></td><td>{0}</td><td>{1}</td><td>{2}</td>
    <td>{3}</td><td><a href='{6}'>{4}</a></td><td>{5}</td></tr>",
    row[5].ToString(), row[1].ToString(), row[2].ToString(),
    row[4].ToString(), row[0].ToString(), row[3].ToString(),
    row[10].ToString(), getImageRef(row[9].ToString()));
  bAltRow = !bAltRow;
}
messages.AppendFormat(@"</table>");
```

To complete the `Display()` method, we will set the `Text` property of the literal
control named `_output` to the `StringBuilder` object message that we have been
building. There is some additional error handling and object disposal included as
part of the overall code flow.

```
            this.EnsureChildControls();
            this._output.Text = messages.ToString();
        }
        catch (Exception ex)
        {
            this.EnsureChildControls();
            this._output.Text = "Error: " + ex.Message.ToString();
        }
        finally
        {
            mQuery.Dispose();
        }
    }
    catch
    {
        this.EnsureChildControls();
        this._output.Text = "Error: Please specify a Search Service
        Application.";
    }
}
```

The views also reference a simple method that will display an appropriate document icon for the specified file extension.

```
private string getImageRef(string extension)
{
  string image = "";
  switch (extension){
    case "DOCX":
      image = "/_layouts/images/icdocx.gif";
      break;
    case "XLSX":
      image = "/_layouts/images/icdocx.gif";
      break;
    case "PDF":
      image = "/_layouts/images/ICLOG.GIF";
      break;
    default:
      image = "/_layouts/images/ICLOG.GIF";
      break;
  }
  return image;
}
```

Display DocVault Listings Web Part

As we have seen, the DocVault Listings Web Part supports both a **DocVault Recently Added** view and a **DocVault Edited by Me** view. The rendered screenshots are shown as follows:

DocVault Recently Added

Type	Site	Customer	Account	Document ID	Name	Modified
	Sales Orders	Test Client	30029	SALESORDERS-1-139	Sales Order	9/11/2011 11:03:03 PM
	Sales Orders	B Client	2002	SALESORDERS-1-138	Sales Order	9/11/2011 11:02:33 PM
	Sales Orders	C Client	2004	SALESORDERS-1-137	Sales Order	9/11/2011 11:02:07 PM
	Sales Orders	D Client	2005	SALESORDERS-1-136	Sales Order	9/11/2011 11:01:36 PM
	Sales Orders	C Client	2004	SALESORDERS-1-135	Sales Order	9/11/2011 11:01:04 PM
	Sales Orders	B Client	2003	SALESORDERS-1-134	Sales Order	9/11/2011 11:00:33 PM
	Sales Orders	A Client	2002	SALESORDERS-1-133	Sales Order	9/11/2011 11:00:12 PM
	Invoices	SD Industries	29928	INVOICES-1-165	Invoice	9/11/2011 10:58:12 PM
	Invoices	Test Landing	02029	INVOICES-1-167	Invoice	9/11/2011 10:57:49 PM
	Invoices	SD Industries	2002929	INVOICES-1-166	Invoices	9/11/2011 10:57:26 PM
	Invoices	BG Industries	2009	INVOICES-1-170	Invoice	9/11/2011 10:57:01 PM
	Invoices	Gemstone	20029	INVOICES-1-169	Invoice	9/11/2011 10:56:32 PM
	Invoices	Peach Tree Industries	010299	INVOICES-1-168	Invoice	9/11/2011 10:56:03 PM
	Invoices	TrackStar	02988	INVOICES-1-172	Invoice	9/11/2011 10:55:38 PM
	Invoices	Sampson United	020002	INVOICES-1-171	Invoice	9/11/2011 10:54:52 PM

DocVault Edited By Me						
Type	Site	Customer	Account	Document ID	Name	Modified
📄	Invoices	Acme	12345	INVOICES-1-37	Invoice_201001.docx	9/4/2011 9:03:57 PM
📄	Invoices	Acme	12345	INVOICES-1-40	Invoice_201004.docx	9/4/2011 9:04:26 PM
📄	Invoices	Acme	12345	INVOICES-1-41	Invoice_201005.docx	9/4/2011 9:04:36 PM
📄	Invoices	Acme	12345	INVOICES-1-42	Invoice_201006.docx	9/4/2011 9:04:45 PM
📄	Invoices	Acme	12345	INVOICES-1-43	Invoice_201007.docx	9/4/2011 9:04:55 PM
📄	Invoices	Acme	12345	INVOICES-1-45	Invoice_201009.docx	9/4/2011 9:05:14 PM
📄	Invoices	Acme	12345	INVOICES-1-46	Invoice_201010.docx	9/4/2011 9:05:23 PM
📄	Invoices	Acme	12345	INVOICES-1-47	Invoice_201011.docx	9/4/2011 9:05:33 PM
📄	Invoices	Acme	12345	INVOICES-1-48	Invoice_201012.docx	9/4/2011 9:05:42 PM
📄	Invoices	Acme	12345	INVOICES-1-49	Invoice_201013.docx	9/4/2011 9:05:52 PM
📄	Invoices	Acme	12345	INVOICES-1-50	Invoice_201014.docx	9/4/2011 9:06:01 PM
📄	Invoices	Acme	12345	INVOICES-1-51	Invoice_201015.docx	9/4/2011 9:06:10 PM
📄	Invoices	Acme	12345	INVOICES-1-52	Invoice_201016.docx	9/4/2011 9:06:20 PM
📄	Invoices	Acme	12345	INVOICES-1-53	Invoice_201017.docx	9/4/2011 9:06:29 PM
📄	Invoices	Acme	12345	INVOICES-1-54	Invoice_201018.docx	9/4/2011 9:06:39 PM

Enhancing the Document ID redirect

The Document ID service was added to the SharePoint Server 2010 to help with the retrieval of documents in large or complex systems. It adds a field to the Document content type that provides a unique identity to that document within the site collection. This is very helpful in cases where documents move around between libraries or sites within the site collection, perhaps via a workflow, or in cases like the solution here where there are perhaps tens of thousands of documents to be sifted through.

In addition to adding the additional field and maintaining the value assignment process, there is also an additional Web Part provided that supports a form that allows the user to provide the unique Document ID. It also sends it to a redirect service that will load the document no matter where it is stored within that site collection.

The feature is nearly flawless when used within a single site collection, but in most organizations, enterprise content cannot (and should not) be stored within a single site collection. In order to get the feature to work with multiple site collections, we need to direct the request to the appropriate site collection.

Enhanced DocID redirect approach

The enhanced DocID redirect Web Part will provide a simple mechanism to direct the user's lookup to the redirect page in the right site collection. The standard Doc ID redirection page is available here: `/_layouts/DocIdRedir.aspx?ID=[Document ID]`.

A simple, but effective, way of maintaining the DocID destinations would be to use a simple linked list on the main Document Vault home site. That list can be created with a List Definition and List Instance in Visual Studio, or configured manually in the browser. In addition to the standard columns, an additional column was added named `isActive` to allow destinations to be deactivated if needed.

The Web Part will use the Client OM to read the `DocumentIDLocations` list and load all active locations into a drop-down box. The drop-down in combination with the Document ID textbox will form the link needed for the Document ID's redirect page.

Creating an enhanced DocID redirect script

As this will be done using the Client OM, we will create an HTML file to contain our script. Within that file we will start by adding a container for our code. The display for this Web Part is very simple, it includes a `div` container named `DocIDRedirect`, a `span` container named `DocLocations` that will contain the rendered drop-down with locations, a standard input box named `DocumentID`, and then an image link used for a Submit button.

```
<div id="DocIDRedirect" class="s4-search">
  <span id="DocLocations">
  </span>
  <br />
  <input type="text" id="DocumentID" value="" maxlength="20"
   title="DocumentID" class="ms-sbplain" size="120"/>
  <div style="float:right">
    <a href="javascript:docRedirect();">
    <img border="0" class="srch-gosearchimg" alt="Go"
     src="/_layouts/images/DocIdLookup.png"></a>
  </div>
</div>
```

We will now create the `script` block to hold our ECMAScript and add in the `ExecuteOrDelayUntilScriptLoaded` call which will wait for the page to fully load before calling the `loadDocumentIDLocations` method.

```
<script type="text/ecmascript" language="ecmascript">
  ExecuteOrDelayUntilScriptLoaded(loadDocumentIDLocations,
    "sp.js");
</script>
</div>
```

Within the `script` block we will now add in the referenced
`loadDocumentIDLocations()` method. This method will connect to the
list and execute a query to load any active Document ID locations.

```
function loadDocumentIDLocations() {
  var listTitle = "DocumentIDLocations";
  var context = SP.ClientContext.get_current();
  var list = context.get_web().get_lists().getByTitle(listTitle);
  var camlQuery = new SP.CamlQuery();
  camlQuery.set_viewXml("<ViewFields><FielfRef Name='isActive'
   /><FieldRef Name='URL' /></ViewFields><Where>
   <Eq><FieldRef Name='isActive'/><ValueType='Boolean'>1</Value>
   </Eq></Where><OrderBy>
   <FieldRef Name='URLwMenu' Ascending='True' /></OrderBy>");

  this.listItems = list.getItems(camlQuery);
  context.load(listItems);
  context.executeQueryAsync(ReadListItemSucceeded,
    ReadListItemFailed);
}
```

If the query was successful, the `ReadListItemSuceeded()` method will be called.
From here we can now create the `docSelect` drop-down and populate it with the
returned options. When the control is fully populated, the resulting HTML will be
set within the `DocLocations` container previously created.

```
function ReadListItemSucceeded(sender, args) {
  comboContents = "<select id='docSelect' style='width:200px'>";
  var items = listItems.getEnumerator();

  while (items.moveNext()) {
    var listItem = items.get_current();
    listItem.get_item('URL').get_description());
    comboContents += "<option value='" +
      listItem.get_item('URL').get_url() + "'>" +
      listItem.get_item('URL').get_description() + "</option>";
  }
  comboContents += "</select>";
  document.getElementById("DocLocations").innerHTML =
    comboContents;
}
```

If the query was not successful, the `ReadListItemFailed()` method will be called and an `alert` with the exception and stack trace will be displayed.

```
function ReadListItemFailed(sender, args) {
  alert('Error: ' + args.get_message() + '\n' +
    args.get_stackTrace());
}
```

The final method is the `docRedirect()` method that is called when a user clicks on the image to submit the form. This is a simple call to redirect the user to the selected Document ID location and supplies the `DocumentID` value specified by the user.

```
function docRedirect() {
  location.href= document.getElementById("docSelect").value +
    document.getElementById("DocumentID").value;
}
```

When the file is complete, save it and upload it to a document library on the site. For the purpose of this example, I have uploaded the script to a library named `Scripts`.

Configuring the DocID redirect Web Part

With the script uploaded to the site, it is now available to be used within the Web Part on the page.

To add the Web Part to the Document Vault home page:

1. Browse to the page you want to add the Web Part to.
2. Click on the **Site Actions** menu and select **Edit Page**.
3. Within the top-right zone, click on the **Add a Web Part** option.
4. Within the **Media and Content** category, select the **Content Editor** Web Part.
5. Click on the **Add** button.
6. Provide a **Title** such as `Find by Document ID`.
7. For the **Content Link**, provide a link to the script that was uploaded.
8. After all of the desired properties are set, click on the **OK** button to apply the changes.

Displaying the DocID redirect

The rendered DocID redirect Web Part is shown in the following screenshot:

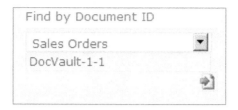

Summary

This section leveraged both the Server and Client OMs, along with SharePoint's ECM features, to create a robust business solution.

The customizations are grouped as follows:

- Browser based configuration:
    - **Site collection**: Provision site collections to hold our solution
    - **List instance**: Provision lists to hold our content
    - **Content Editor Web Part (CEWP)**: Use the Content Query Web Part to display our content
    - **Content type**: Define content types to describe our content
    - **Site column**: Define site columns for use with the related content types
    - **Content type hub**: Use the content type hub to synchronize content types to subscribing site collections
    - **Content Organizer**: Use the Content Organizer and configured rules to move content from the Drop Off library to libraries in one or more site collections
- Visual Studio 2010:
    - **Custom Web Part**: Use the Search API to load content for display in a custom Web Part that can aggregate relevant content from within the system.

These solutions provide examples of how to leverage SharePoint 2010's ECM features to provide a robust solution that scales for extremely large scenarios, while still providing an intuitive user experience.

4
Building an Engaging Community Site

Organizations today are looking for ways to increase collaboration and to provide more self-help resources through the use of tools like SharePoint. Thanks to the built-in Team Site template, it can be fairly easy to build a department-level collaboration site, but there is currently no template that is optimized for use as a true community collaboration site where the content is less structured, more conversational, and where the group will evolve over time, unlike your traditional department site.

This chapter will attempt to address the challenges of using a Team Site for community collaboration so that you can build a community site that can keep people engaged and incorporate the collaboration levels that everyone is looking for.

Community sites can be used to drive collaboration and self-help around a specific topic or system. Examples could include business topics like Lean, Six Sigma, or other process improvement methodologies, or for system support for various ERP, HRIS, or IT systems. The management, education, and governance of SharePoint itself make for a good community site focus, and will be the focus of this chapter. Using this solution as a template though, there could be numerous community sites created for an organization.

The community sites can provide a much better collaboration platform, and also can provide user training and a help platform as well. The key difference for a community site is moving away from the default content of a Team Site which focuses primarily on shared documents and a team calendar and instead focuses on more dynamic and social features focused on the community content. When done properly, people throughout the organization will be willing participants and can help provide that support which better utilizes the company's resources and potentially provide more relevant information. Community sites should be the future of collaboration and perhaps for IT system support.

Just like the Effective Intranet covered in *Chapter 1, Building an Effective Intranet*, it is essential to start this process by defining what the goals for the site are, followed by defining the information architecture, content, and feature strategy.

Most community sites have varying levels of formality to the content. The formality of the content may be decided upon based on who can contribute content, whether it needs to be reviewed and approved, and whether it is retained in the system long term. On the informal side it could be completely informal collaboration with a very wide range of collaborators using tools like a note board, a threaded discussion list, or perhaps a list of helpful links. This is true user-generated content that can be added quickly and easily, though it may not be as complete or 'authoritative' as more formal content. Moving more towards the formal side, you may also see edited and approved Frequently Asked Question type lists or system and process documentation. As the community fills with information, it becomes more important to start highlighting popular or useful content.

This chapter will provide an overview of configuration steps needed to create a base Community site template, along with example customizations that can be created to provide dynamic and relevant content, which is a key ingredient to building an engaging Community Site solution. The covered solutions include:

- Enterprise Wikis
- Content Rollups
- Community Leaders Group

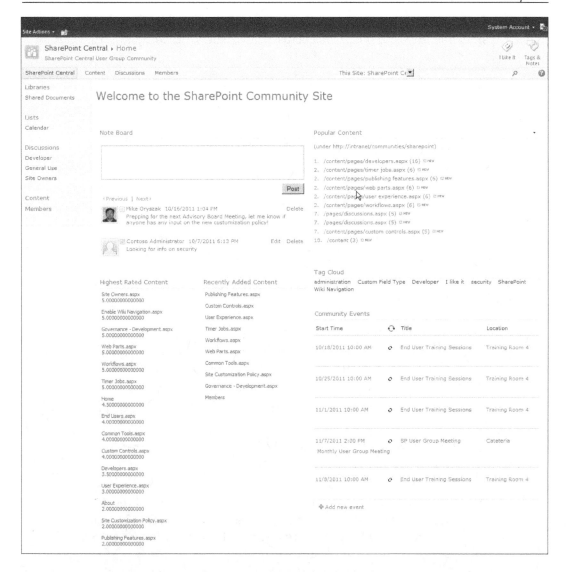

Creating the Community Site

To get started we will need to provision a new site collection to hold our solution, activate the supporting features, and create a landing page to support our community.

In this case I have selected a Team Site template because it is a good generic building block for sites like this, and it can also be used to create Web Templates that can be used to provision additional sites in the future.

See *Choosing a Site Template* section in *Chapter 1, Building an Effective Intranet* for additional background information on the available site templates.

Activating supporting features

After choosing a site template and creating the site collection, the next step is to activate the initial features needed to support the Community site. The robust feature deployment and activation system supported in SharePoint makes it very easy to fine tune the functionality available within a site, since individual features can be activated as they are required. In many cases these features may already be activated by default, depending on your settings for the web application and overall farm.

Following is a list of the features that are required to be activated on the site being configured for this solution:

- Site Collection features:
    - **Document ID Service**: It assigns IDs to documents in the Site Collection, which can be used to retrieve items independent of their current location.
    - **Search Server Web Parts**: This feature uploads all web parts required for Search Center.
    - **SharePoint Server Standard Site Collection features**: It provides features such as user profiles and search, included in the SharePoint Server Standard License.
    - **SharePoint Server Enterprise Site Collection features**: It provides features such as InfoPath Forms Services, Visio Services, Access Services, and Excel Services Application, included in the SharePoint Server Enterprise License.
    - **SharePoint Server Publishing Infrastructure**: It provides centralized libraries, content types, master pages, and page layouts and enables page scheduling and other publishing functionality for a site collection.

- Site features:

  - ° **SharePoint Server Standard Site Collection features**: It provides features such as user profiles and search, included in the SharePoint Server Standard License.

  - ° **SharePoint Server Enterprise Site Collection features**: It provides features such as InfoPath Forms Services, Visio Services, Access Services, and Excel Services Application, included in the SharePoint Server Enterprise License.

  - ° **SharePoint Server Publishing**: It is used to create a Web page library as well as supporting libraries to create and publish pages based on page layouts.

For anyone that is not familiar with the publishing features, it is important to understand that the Document Libraries setup for publishing, including the resources provisioned when the feature is activated such as the Style Library, will require that all changes be fully published for non-administrators to be able to view the most recent changes. If changes are made to pages, scripts, images, or CSS stylesheets included in any of these libraries and are not fully published, you will see unexpected behaviors such as 404 errors, out of date content, or miscellaneous unexpected SharePoint page level errors.

Creating and configuring the community landing page

With the Publishing features enabled at both the Site Collection and web level, we can now create and configure our landing page.

From anywhere on the community site:

1. Click **Site Actions** menu, and select the **New Page** item.
2. Provide a title for the page.
3. Click the **Create** button.

When the page is created it will open in edit mode and be ready for configuration. The next task is to set the appropriate page layout. In the **Page** tab of the ribbon is an action for the **Page Layout**. Within the selection panel, a list of options will be displayed by category with an included thumbnail. The **Welcome Page** category includes some great landing pages, and for this one we will select the **Blank Web Part page** option as shown in the following screenshot:

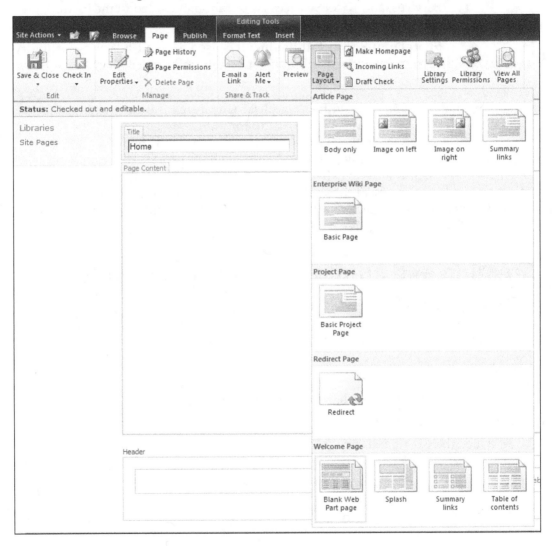

4. Next, we will want to set the new page as the site's Homepage. In the **Page** tab of the ribbon is the **Make Homepage** action, as shown in following screenshot. Click this action to set the new page as the site's homepage.

Site Permissions

Permissions management is one of the things that is typically different when working with community sites. Where a traditional department site is tied to a specific department and likely has an Active Directory security group, the community site is meant to be cross-functional including people from throughout the organization. Making that collaboration easy, especially for new members, often means taking a completely different approach.

The approach that I typically take is to identify the top most Active Directory groups that apply and then grant them Contributor permission level. That could be something like <my domain>\domain users which is a standard security group that will include all domain users. Letting everyone contribute by default will make the site easier to maintain and also better support collaboration and innovation.

Community members

One way to profile community advocates and members from throughout the organization is to find a way to list out the community's members. A great way to do this is to define a user profile property that can track the communities that the person is associated with. The advantage of this is that it will link the user to the community within their user profile as well as list them as a member on the community site. This one field can be used to support all of the communities throughout the organization so it should only be created once. The great thing about this property is that it can be used to help find people within the user profiles, but also it can be used to display the members within the community site itself. In this section we will define the custom user profile property and then create a custom page that lists people associated with the community.

Creating Communities User Profile Property

The User Profiles Properties are stored and maintained within the User Profile Service Application. This information is available from any site collection within the web applications associated with the service application.

The properties we will create should be available for everyone to see, but in other cases there may be varying levels of visibility and overall behavior. Creating a new property requires thought and planning to ensure that the desired privacy, security, and behaviors are available.

To create the User Profile properties:

1. From **Central Administration**, browse to the **User Profile Service Application**.

2. On the **Manage User Properties** screen, click on the **New Property** menu item as shown in the following screenshot:

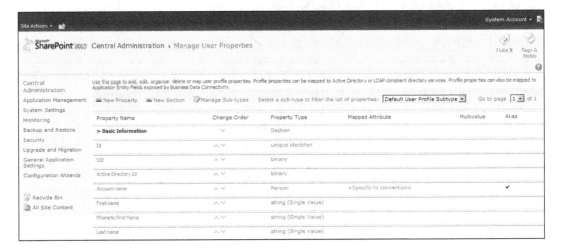

3. Set the **Name** field to **Communities**.
4. Set the **Display Name** field to **Communities**.
5. Set the **Type** field to **String** (Multi Value).
6. Set the **Length** field to **250**.
7. Set the **Multivalue Separator** field to **Semicolon**.
8. Ensure the **Default User Profile Subtype** value is set to **Yes**.
9. Set the **Description** field to **Community Site Membership**.
10. Set the **Policy Setting** field to **Optional**.
11. Set the **Default Privacy Setting** to **Everyone**.
12. Set the **Edit Settings** field to **Allow users to edit values for this property**.
13. Set the **Show in profile** field to **Yes**.
14. Set the **Show in Edit Details** page to **Yes**.

Mapping Communities as a Managed Property

To make it easier to retrieve people in specified groups we will identify the Communities property as a Managed Property.

To create the mapping:

1. From **Central Administration**, browse to the **Search Service Application**.
2. Click on the **Metadata Properties** link under the **Queries and Results** heading.
3. Provide a **Property** name value such as **Communities** and a description.
4. Under the **Mappings to crawled properties** section, click on the **Add Mapping** button and search for the **Communities** field identified in the content type.
5. Select the **People:Communities**(Text) and click on the **OK** button.

Configuring the Members Page

The Members page will display a listing of all of the group members using SharePoint's People Search and the People Core Results Web Part to execute a set query that looks at the Communities field previously defined.

Creating the Members Page

To create the members page:

1. Click on the **Site Actions** menu, and select the **New Page** item.

2. Provide a title for the page.

3. Click on the **Create** button.

Adding the People Search Core Results Web Part

To add the People Search Core Results Web Part to the page:

1. Click on the **Insert** tab of the Ribbon.

2. Select the **Web Parts** action.

3. Select the **Search** category.

4. Select the **People Search Core Results** Web Part.

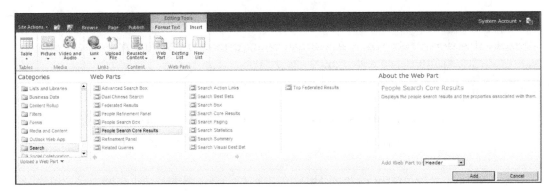

Configuring Members Search Query

To configure the pre-set members search query:

1. Edit the **People Core Results** Web Part properties.

2. Under the **Display Properties** group, change the **Default Results Sorting** to **Name**.

3. Set the **Results Per Page** value to **20**.

4. If custom properties need to be displayed, they need to be added to the **Fetched Properties** field.

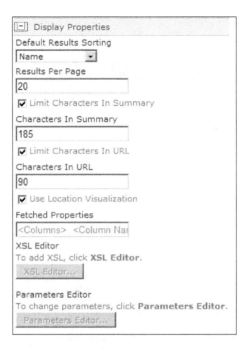

5. Under the **Results Query Options** group, change the **Cross-Web Part query ID**.

6. Change the **Fixed Keyword Query** to **Communities:"SharePoint"**.

7. Under the **Appearance** group, change the **Chrome Type** field to **None**.

8. Click on the **OK** button.

The **Fixed Keyword Query** value added in step 6 will do a managed property search for the **Communities** field and look for matches with the value "SharePoint" which is the name of this community.

The final rendered view is displayed as shown in the following screenshot:

Configuring social web parts

The social features included with SharePoint Server 2010 are intended to support collaboration and increase user engagement. Both the Note Board and Tag Cloud web parts are included to help support those social interactions.

Note Board Web Part

The Note Board Web Part allows users to pose a simple note such as a question they need help with, or some other note that may benefit the community. Any notes saved will be tied to the URL of the page it is on, so it is important to understand that, unlike a discussion board, there should be some thought put into which pages the note board is prominently placed on.

To add a Note Board Web Part to the front page of the site:

1. Browse to the homepage of the community site.
2. Click on the **Site Actions** menu and select the **Edit Page** option.
3. Select the **Insert ribbon** tab.
4. Select the **Social Collaboration** category.
5. Select the **Note Board** Web Part as displayed in the following screenshot:

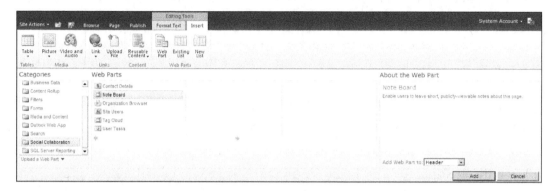

6. For the **Add Web Part to** option, select **Header**. Click on the **Add** button.

An example of the Note Board is displayed in the following screenshot:

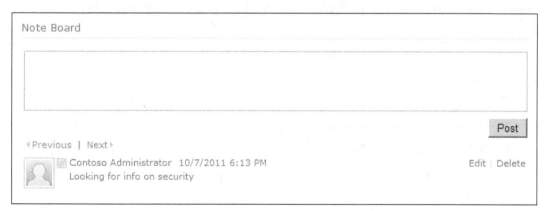

Tagging and Tag Clouds

The Tagging and Tag Clouds features introduced with SharePoint Server 2010 are powered by the Managed Metadata Services and allow users to apply tags to any content including pages, documents, or list items. Users can tag the item using any term they choose, but they are also given tag recommendations based on what other people tagged the document with. This informal meta-data process provides a lot of flexibility, better supporting informal or dynamic content, but it also provides a much more personalized experience which users tend to appreciate.

All tags that a user sets will be available to them in their profile page and MySites, and users also have the ability to subscribe to tags so that they receive updates when that tag is used. This is great for cases where maybe they are a Subject Matter Expert (SME) on a topic or perhaps a Product Manager responsible for a given product.

The Tag Cloud web part that ships with SharePoint Server 2010 offers three views to filter the available tags:

- By current user
- By all users
- Under the current URL by all users

The appropriate selection will depend on the context of how you want to use the information. In the case of our community site, we want to make it easy for people to find information so we want people to be able to leverage the tags of other users on this particular site.

To add the Tag Cloud Web Part to the community site:

1. Browse to the homepage of the community site.
2. Click on the **Site Actions** menu and select the **Edit Page** option.
3. Select the **Insert ribbon** tab.
4. Select the **Social Collaboration** category.

5. Select the **Tag Cloud** Web Part as displayed in the following screenshot:

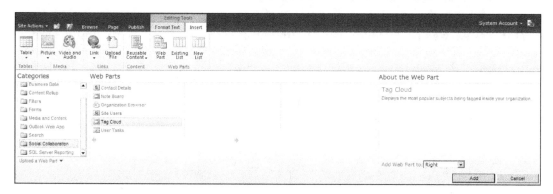

6. For the **Add Web Part to** option, select **Right**.
7. Click on the **Add** button.

By default the Web Part will display the current user's tags. To change that simply edit the Web Part settings and change the **Show Tags** option to **Under the current URL for all users** as displayed in the following screenshot:

Configuring Rollup Web Parts

It is important that we continue to try and find effective ways to surface content so that it is as easy as possible for users to find and use the content. To do that we are going to leverage two additional Web Parts available in SharePoint Server that can assist here. The Web Parts are:

- Web Analytics Web Part
- Content Query Web Part

Web Analytics Web Part – Frequently Accessed Content

The Web Analytics Web Part leverages the Usage and Web Analytics system to provide content reporting to your authors and end users. In the past it has been difficult to provide an accurate list of Frequently Accessed Content, but this Web Part provides that much needed information.

It is important to understand that this is pre-processed information that is generated based on the schedule configured for the Web Analytics reporting. This allows it to execute very fast, but with default settings the content may be up to 24 hours out of date, so new content may not be displayed.

To configure the Web Analytics Web Part:

1. Browse to the homepage of the community site.
2. Click on the **Site Actions** menu and select the **Edit Page** option.
3. Select the **Insert** ribbon tab.
4. Select the **Content Rollup** category.
5. Select the **Web Analytics Web Part** as displayed in the following screenshot:

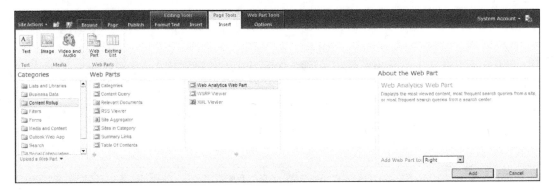

6. For the **Add Web Part to** option, select **Top Right**.

7. Click on the **Add button**.

8. Edit the **Web Part** settings.

9. Change the **Information to Display** option to **Most Viewed Content**.

10. Ensure that the **Site Scope** option is set to **This Site and Subsites**.

11. Ensure that the **Period** option is set to **Proceeding 30 Days**.

12. Select the **Show Frequency** option.

13. Select the **Show Popularity Rank** option.

14. Select the **Show Popularity Rank** Trend option.

15. Under the **Appearance** section, change the **Title** field to **Popular Content**.

An example of the configured Web Part is displayed in the following screenshot:

```
Popular Content

(under http://intranet/communities/sharepoint)

1.   /content/pages/developers.aspx (16)  ⬚ NEW
2.   /content/pages/timer jobs.aspx (6)  ⬚ NEW
2.   /content/pages/publishing features.aspx (6)  ⬚ NEW
2.   /content/pages/web parts.aspx (6)  ⬚ NEW
2.   /content/pages/user experience.aspx (6)  ⬚ NEW
2.   /content/pages/workflows.aspx (6)  ⬚ NEW
7.   /pages/discussions.aspx (5)  ⬚ NEW
7.   /pages/discussions.aspx (5)  ⬚ NEW
7.   /content/pages/custom controls.aspx (5)  ⬚ NEW
10.  /content (3)  ⬚ NEW
```

Content Query Web Part – New Content

The Content Query Web Part allows you to do simple content rollups within a site collection. We are going to configure one that can be used to highlight new pages that are added to the site.

To configure the Content Query Web Part:

1. Browse to the homepage of the community site.

2. Click on the **Site Actions** menu and select the **Edit Page** option.

3. Select the **Insert ribbon** tab.

4. Select the **Content Rollup** category.

5. Select the **Content Query** as displayed in the following screenshot:

6. For the **Add Web Part to** option, select **Right**.

7. Click the **Add** button.

8. Edit the **Web Part** settings.

9. Under the **Query** section, **List Type** grouping, set the **Show items from this list type** field to the **Pages Library** option.

10. Under the **Presentation** section, **Grouping and Sorting grouping**, set the **Sort items by** field to the **Created** option.

11. Ensure that the **Show items in descending order** option is selected.

12. Under the **Styles** grouping, set the **Item Style** field to **Title, description, and document icon**.

13. Under the **Appearance** section, set the **Title** field to **Recently Added Content**.

14. Click on the **OK** button.

An example of the configured Web Part is displayed in the following screenshot:

Content Query Web Part – Highly Rated Content

Next we will add and configure another Content Query Web Part that will highlight the highest rated pages that are added to the site.

To configure the Content Query Web Part:

1. Browse to the homepage of the community site.
2. Click the **Site Actions** menu and select the **Edit Page** option.
3. Select the **Insert** ribbon tab.
4. Select the **Content Rollup** category.
5. Select the **Content Query** as displayed in the following screenshot:

6. For the **Add Web Part to** option, select **Top Left**.
7. Click on the **Add** button.
8. Edit the **Web Part** settings.
9. Under the **Query** section, **List Type** grouping, set the **Show items from this list type** field to the **Pages Library** option.
10. Under the **Presentation** section, **Grouping and Sorting** grouping, set the **Sort items by** field to the **Rating (0-5)** option.
11. Ensure that the **Show** items in descending order option is selected.
12. Under the **Styles** grouping, set the **Item Style** field to **Title, description, and document icon**.
13. Under the **Fields to Display** grouping, **Description** field, add **Rating (0-5)**; to the field listing to show the current rating for the content.
14. Under the **Appearance** section, set the **Title** field to **Recently Added Content**.
15. Click on the **OK** button.

An example of the configured Web Part is displayed in the following screenshot:

Creating an Enterprise Wiki

Using Wikis is a great way to collaborate on content within SharePoint. While most people still think in terms of documents and pages, there are a number of advantages to using Wikis over individual documents or pages.

These advantages include:

- They can support a more collaborative process and tap into the collective knowledge of a wider range of content contributors
- They have the ability to easily link from one document to another through page markup
- They have the ability to easily see what changes were made and by who without the need to use **Track Changes**

The Enterprise Wikis feature, introduced with SharePoint Server 2010, provides some much needed advances over the standard Wiki features including the ability to integrate other Web Parts or SharePoint content within the Wiki content. While the page editing and markup are the exact same, there are page layout changes that provide much better support organizing large sets of content. The features include Page Ratings, Wiki Categories, making it easier to tag and relate pages, and also Metadata Navigation.

Additional information on SharePoint 2010's Enterprise Wikis is available here: `http://technet.microsoft.com/en-us/library/ee721051.aspx`

This section will detail the recommended steps for:

- Configuring the Enterprise Wiki on our community site
- Explaining the use of categories
- Activating the Metadata Navigation feature
- Configuring a navigation scheme that will make it easier to find the content

Configuring the Enterprise Wiki sub-site

Next we will create a sub-site to hold our Enterprise Wiki content.

When configuring a Wiki, it is important to consider where to place that content. It is possible to simply create a Wiki library on a given site, but when considering site topology, in many cases it is more beneficial to create the Wiki as a sub-site in order to segment and manage the content separately if needed, but also in order to optimize content rollups and search.

To create an Enterprise Wiki as a sub-site:

1. From the community site, click on the **Site Actions** menu.
2. Select the **New Site** option.
3. Select the **Enterprise Wiki** option.
4. In the right margin, click on the **More Options** button.
5. Provide a value for the **Title** field.
6. Provide a value for the **Description** field.
7. Provide a value for the **URL** field.
8. Ensure the **Use the same permissions as parent site?** option is selected which will ensure that users have the same permissions on the sub-site.
9. Under **Navigation Inheritance**, select the **Yes** option which will ensure that the navigation is consistent between the two sites.
10. Click on the **Create** button to create the site.

An example of the form for creating an Enterprise Wiki is available in the following screenshot:

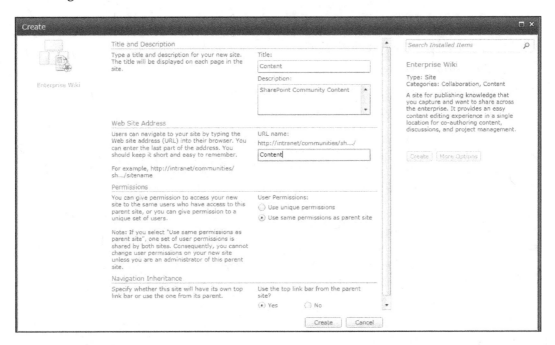

Use of Categories

The categories make it easy to organize and locate your content. Where most site fields are editable only within the library, the Enterprise Wiki has the category field available directly on the Wiki page. When editing a page the taxonomy field is enabled and new categories can be added or selected. An example is shown in the following screenshot:

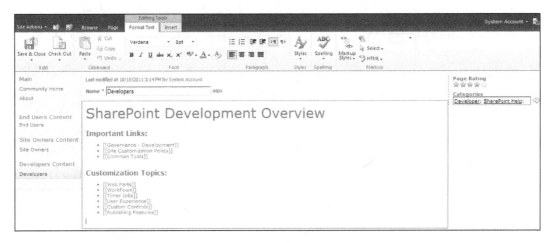

When browsing the pages, any identified categories will be displayed. Clicking one of the category values will lead to a special **Category** filtering page that will display all wiki pages in the library that match that category value.

It is important to keep in mind that the identified categories are stored in the Term Store and will not be surfaced through the Tag Cloud Web Part previously configured. If users want pages to show up in the Tag Cloud, the pages also have to be tagged using the tagging feature.

Metadata Navigation

As the number of pages and the amount of content grows, finding that content in a large Wiki can get very challenging. One of the great features added with SharePoint Server 2010 is the Metadata Navigation feature. This feature can be used to browse items based on the category metadata. This feature, however, is not enabled by default, so unless it is included as part of an automated site provisioning process, it will need to be enabled manually.

Activating the Metadata Navigation feature

To activate the Metadata Navigation feature:

1. From the **Enterprise Wiki** site, click on **Site Actions**.

2. Select the **Site Settings** option.

3. Under the **Site Actions** group, click on the **Manage Site Features** link.

4. Browse to the **Metadata Navigation** and **Filtering** feature and click on the **Activate** button.

Configuring Metadata Navigation for Enterprise Wiki Library

With the feature now activated on the site, we can configure its use within the Enterprise Wiki library.

To configure Metadata Navigation on the library:

1. From one of the Wiki pages, select the **Page** ribbon tab and select the **View All Pages** action as shown in the following screenshot:

2. Select the **Library Settings** action as shown in the following screenshot:

3. Under the **General Settings** category, click on the **Metadata navigation settings** link as shown in the following screenshot:

4. Select the **Folders and Wiki Categories** nodes.

5. Click on the **Add** Button.

6. To complete the **Configure Key Filters** section, select the desired fields and click on the **Add** button.

7. Click on the **OK** button when finished to save your changes.

The **Manage Navigation Settings** screen is displayed in the following screenshot:

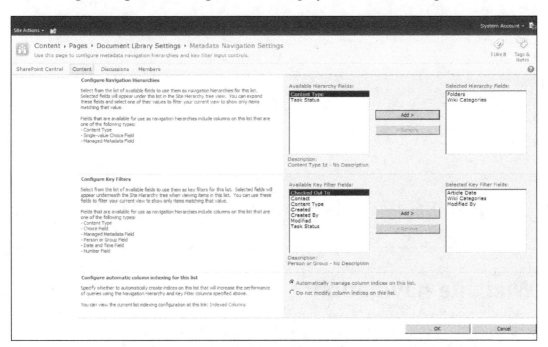

Using the feature

With Metadata Navigation now configured, whenever you are on a view page within the library you will see a Category navigation control added to the left side below the standard QuickLaunch navigation. Selecting a tag will filter down the related Wiki Pages associated with that tag, providing a quick and effective way of finding content. As you will see in the Site Navigation section that follows, it is possible to add navigation nodes to the top most common or important categories.

You will also noticed that the Key Filters control is also displayed on the left-hand side allowing for advanced filtering of any fields that were configured. This is especially helpful when looking for content by a specific author, or perhaps based on dates.

An example of the Metadata Navigation is displayed in the following screenshot:

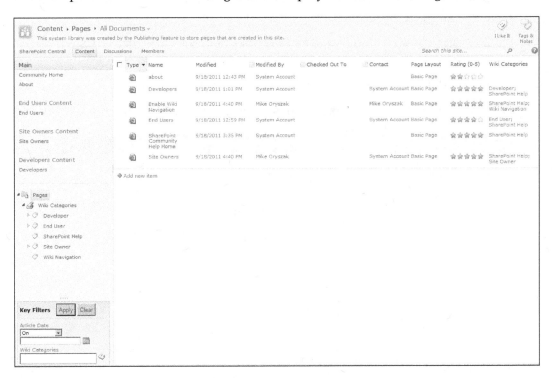

Wiki site navigation

In addition to the Metadata Navigation covered in the previous section, it is also important to consider the navigation employed with the standard Quicklaunch navigation when browsing the wiki pages. This will give you the ability to highlight very important and 'authoritative' pages, in addition to browsing and filtering by category.

The normal navigation settings page available by navigating through Site Actions, Navigation supports having Wiki pages added to the navigation automatically, which may work fine with small Wikis, but does not work well if you have dozens or hundreds of Wiki pages. For most Wikis established for free form collaboration, generally uncheck the **Show Pages** option for the Current Navigation section. This means that any navigation would have to be configured manually. This should be reserved for high level category pages or other very important pages. It does take some on-going maintenance but will result in a much more organized system. The general navigation should be determined by how the content is organized.

Since the purpose of this Wiki is for content relating to SharePoint, a set of categories have been identified:

- Main
- End User
- Site Owner
- Developer

For each of these categories, a Section Heading will be created that links to the main view of the library. This will allow users to click into the library to filter down available pages based on the category or topic. In this example, the heading for Main shows the full library, while the others start by selecting the identified tag.

Main section pages can be linked to directly as well as any other important pages. As new pages are added, the most important ones should be added to the navigation settings, but not too many, as it will eventually get cluttered.

An example of the Navigation Settings is shown in the following screenshot:

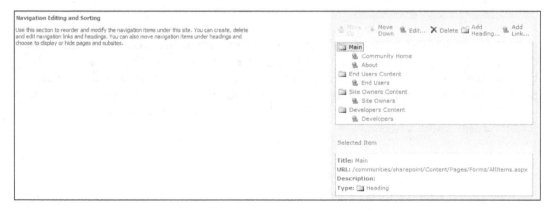

Summary

This section heavily leverages the out of the box Web Parts and features to assemble a rich and interactive community site.

The customizations are grouped as follows:

- Browser-Based Configuration
    - **Site Collection**: To provision a site collection to hold our solution
    - **Content Query Web Part (CQWP)**: To configure the content query Web Part for displaying our content
    - **Web Analytics Web Part**: To configure the web analytics Web Part for displaying relevant content
    - **People Core Results Web Part**: To configure the people core results Web Part to display community membership
    - **Enterprise Wikis**: To configure the enterprise wikis with enhanced navigation functionality
    - **Note Board Web Part**: To configure the note board Web Part for use in supporting community conversations and collaboration
    - **Tag Cloud Web Part**: To configure the tag cloud Web Part in order to help surface relevant content by keyword.

There are a number of additional types of content that may be beneficial to a community that were not covered in detail within this chapter. Items configured, but not covered, include threaded discussions, community events, and community links. The key is to find content that is relevant and make it as easy as possible for participants to contribute.

An effective community site can greatly enhance collaboration, innovation, and provide a foundation for user self-service by giving the users a central place to share content and discuss ideas. It provides a distinct advantage over the use of e-mail because the information is stored in a central repository, versus individual e-mail boxes, which makes it discoverable by anyone with access to the site. Providing an engaging site requires a mix of good content, features, and the ability to personalize it to the community's needs.

5
Building a Site Request and Provisioning System

In many environments, managing site requests and going through the site collection provisioning process is one of the most frequent ongoing tasks. In many cases this is a manual task, and while it is pretty easy to do, it can be tedious and repetitive. There should be some general standards established for how sites should be created, which templates are available, what quotas to apply, and where to put the site collection. In addition, many organizations also have governance policies that require the site request be logged or approved before it can be provisioned in order to meet compliance goals.

Providing an automated site request and provisioning system will:

- Ensure that requests are properly logged
- Ensure that necessary approvals are obtained
- Reduce administrator work by automating the provisioning and configuration of the new site collections

Overview

This chapter will take us through creating a series of solutions that will provide a request and approval system, as well as an automated provisioning and configuration solution.

The following solutions will be created:

- Site request list
- Site request form
- Site provisioning timer job
- Site request custom action

Creating the list

We will create a list called `SiteRequestLog` that can be used to log all of the site requests with the configuration data along with the approval status.

At this point in the book we have created a number of list definitions and instances in Visual Studio. I believe this task should be well understood by this point, so I will not go into the step-by-step process for this solution. If you skipped over the other sections and are not sure how to create a list definition and instance, see the *Notification List Definition and List Instance feature* section in *Chapter 1, Building an Effective Intranet*, or the *Master Delegation Tracking List* section in *Chapter 2, Building an Out of Office Delegation Solution*.

The `SiteRequestLog` list needed to support this solution requires the following fields:

Column	Type
Title	Single line of text
Description	Single line of text
PriOwner	Person
SecOwner	Person
Path	Single line of text
URLName	Single line of text
Template	Choice
Quota	Choice
ApprovedBy	Person
ApprovedDate	Date and time
Status	Choice
CreateDate	Date and time
CreationNotes	Single line of text
Feature *n*	Yes/No

The `Feature` *n* field at the end of the list would be for the specific features you would like to include in the process. For my list and provisioning process, I have included three site collection and three web features that are commonly used. The referenced features listed later can be changed or substituted to meet your needs.

Creating the project

The Create Site timer job will be added to a new project called SPBlueprints. SiteCreation.

To create the initial project:

1. Open Visual Studio 2010.

2. Select **File**, then **New Project**.

3. Browse to the **Installed Templates** and select **Visual C# | SharePoint | 2010**, and then **Empty SharePoint Project**.

4. Enter the project details such as **Name, Location**, and **Solution name**.

5. Within the **SharePoint Customization Wizard**, provide a path to your SharePoint site and then be sure to select the option to **Deploy as a farm solution**.

6. Right-click on the project file and select **Add** then **New Item**.

7. From the template selection screen select the **Empty Element** option.

8. Provide the name CreateSiteTimerJob and click on the **Add** button.

9. Rename the **Feature1** item SiteCreationProcess.

10. Select the SiteCreationProcess.feature item and provide a **Title** and **Description**.

11. Change the **Scope** to **WebApplication** so that the feature is only activated once per web application as shown in the following screenshot:

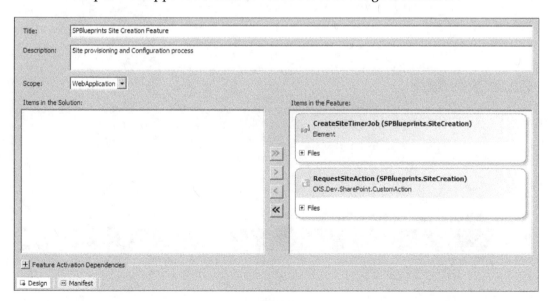

Creating the SiteRequest form

The `SiteRequest` form will be used to log the site requests with the related configuration settings and approval status. As we need this form to be available globally we will use an application page, which is deployed via our feature and available throughout the farm. This will also enable us to show or hide fields as needed and include advanced business logic, which provides significantly more flexibility than standard SharePoint list forms.

To get started we will need to map a folder within the `Layouts` directory.

To map the folder and create the files:

1. Right-click on the project and select the **Add** node then select the **SharePoint "Layouts" Mapped Folder** option.

2. Rename the newly created folder to `SPBlueprintsSiteCreation` without the period.

3. Right-click on the folder and select the **AddNewItem** option.

4. From the SharePoint 2010 category, select the **ApplicationPage** option and provide the name `RequestSite.aspx`.

5. Click on the **Add** button as shown in the following screenshot:

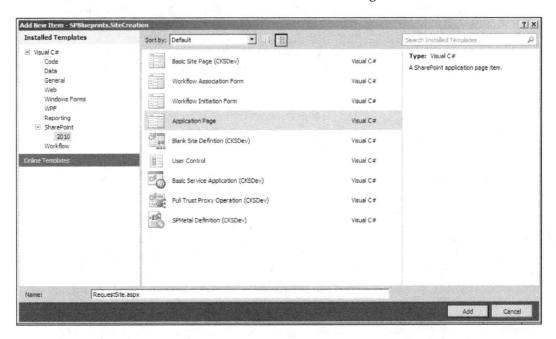

Building the Request Site display page

The standard application page is added to the project, which comprises two files we will now need to build. They are:

- `RequestSite.aspx`: The design surface for controls
- `RequestSite.aspx.cs`: The code behind file for control logic and events

The standard application page template includes the control and resource import statements at the top followed by the content placeholder controls.

To build the Request Site page:

1. Add the page title `Request Site Collection` to the `PlaceHolderPageTitle` control shown as follows:

```
<asp:ContentID="PageTitle"
 ContentPlaceHolderID="PlaceHolderPageTitle" runat="server">
 Request Site Collection
</asp:Content>
```

2. Add the page title `Request Site Collection` to the `PlaceHolderPageTitleInTitleArea` control shown as follows:

```
<asp:ContentID="PageTitleInTitleArea"
 ContentPlaceHolderID="PlaceHolderPageTitleInTitleArea"
 runat="server" >
 Request Site Collection
</asp:Content>
```

3. Next we will build-out the actual form within the `PlaceHolderMain` control. The format and referenced styles will render the form like the standard SharePoint list forms. A label control will be added to provide status and any error messages that need to be displayed.

```
<table class="ms-formtable" style="margin-top:
 8px;"border="0" cellpadding="0" id="formTbl" cellspacing="0"
 width="100%">
<tr>
  <td valign="top" class="ms-formbody" colspan="2" id="Td5">
    <asp:LabelID="Status"runat="server"></asp:Label>
  </td>
</tr>
```

4. The formatting for a simple textfield such as the `Title` property is shown as follows:

```
<tr>
  <td nowrap="true" valign="top" width="165px" class="ms-
  formlabel"><h3 class="ms-
  standardheader"><a name="SPBookmark_Title"></a>
  Site Title</h3>
  </td>
  <td valign="top" class="ms-
  formbody" width="450px" id="SPFieldFile">
    <SharePoint:InputFormTextBox ID="Title"
     runat="server" ControlMode="New" Width="300">
    </SharePoint:InputFormTextBox>
  </td>
</tr>
```

5. The formatting for a person field such as the `PriOwner` property is shown as follows:

```
<tr>
  <td nowrap="true" valign="top" width="165px"
  class="ms-formlabel"><h3 class="ms-standardheader">
  <a name="SPBookmark_PriOwner"></a>Primary Owner</h3>
  </td>
  <td valign="top" class="ms-formbody" width="450px" id="Td2">
    <SharePoint:PeopleEditorID="PriOwner" runat="server"
     MultiSelect="false" MaximumEntities="1" Width="300"/>
  </td>
</tr>
```

6. Our form also requires a drop-down list, which will be used to help preset other list properties such as the managed path, site template, and quota template properties. A standard ASP.NET drop-down control is used as follows:

```
<tr>
  <td nowrap="true" valign="top" width="165px"
  class="ms-formlabel"><h3 class="ms-standardheader">
  <a name="SPBookmark_Path"></a>Site Category</h3>
  </td>
  <td valign="top" class="ms-formbody" width="450px" id="Td3">
    <asp:DropDownList ID="SiteCategory" runat="server"
     Width="300">
    </asp:DropDownList>
  </td>
</tr>
```

7. To handle the selected feature options we will use a standard ASP.NET `CheckBox` control for each of the features available. The form row is shown as follows:

```
<tr>
  <td nowrap="true" valign="top" width="165px"
   class="ms-formlabel"><h3 class="ms-standardheader">
   <a name="SPBookmark_URL"></a>Document ID Service</h3>
  </td>
  <td valign="top" class="ms-formbody" width="450px" id="Td6">
   <asp:CheckBox ID="SiteFeatureDocID" runat="server"/>
  </td>
</tr>
```

8. To submit the form we have included a standard ASP.NET button.

```
    <tr>
        <td colspan="2" align="right">
         <asp:Button ID="Save" runat="server" Text="Save"/>
        </td>
    </tr>
  </table>
</asp:Content>
```

Building the form processing

The code behind this application page is used to handle the form processing during the `Page_Load()` method:

1. We will start by checking to see if the form was posted, and if it was, we will reset the status control and then move into determining some of the configuration settings based on the `SiteCategory` form input field.

```
if (Page.IsPostBack)
{
  this.Status.Text = "";

  try
  {
// Site Categorization
    string quotaTemplate = "";
    string managedPath = "";
    string siteTemplate = "";

    switch (this.SiteCategory.SelectedValue)
    {
```

```
           case"Project Site":
            quotaTemplate = "Project Collab";
            siteTemplate = "Project Site";
            managedPath = "projects/";
            break;
           case"Extranet Site":
            quotaTemplate = "Extranet Collab";
            siteTemplate = "Extranet Site";
            managedPath = "extranet/";
            break;
           default:
            quotaTemplate = "Team Collab";
            siteTemplate = "Team Site";
            managedPath = "sites/";
            break;
         }
```

2. Next we need to connect to the list, which requires that we load the two properties stored in the web application's property bag. With those properties we can establish the required connections.

```
string listName =
 this.Web.Site.WebApplication.Properties["SiteRequestList"].
 ToString();
string listPath =
 this.Web.Site.WebApplication.Properties["SiteRequestSite"].
 ToString();
using (SPSite site = newSPSite(listPath))
{
   using (SPWeb web = site.RootWeb)
{
```

3. When using a `Person` or `Group` field in a SharePoint list, it is necessary to pass in an `SPUser` object when updating the list item. Before we can set the list value we will need to define an `SPUser` object and set it to the form value if one was provided.

```
SPUser userPriOwner = null;
if (this.PriOwner.Accounts.Count > 0)
{
   userPriOwner =
    web.EnsureUser(this.PriOwner.Accounts[0].ToString());
}
```

4. We can now add our list item and set the appropriate field values based on a mixture of our input form and the values that were determined based on internal decisions. For example, the `SiteCategory` selection box drives the field values for the managed path, site template, and quota template. We are also setting the request's status to `Pending Approval`, which is what we have determined is the starting status for our requests. After all of the desired fields are set, we need to call the `Update()` method so that they are saved back to the list.

```
SPListItem newEntry = web.Lists[listName].Items.Add();
newEntry["Title"] = this.Title.Text;
newEntry["Description"] = this.Description.Text;
newEntry["PriOwner"] = userPriOwner;
newEntry["Path"] = managedPath;
newEntry["URLName"] = this.URLName.Text;
newEntry["Template"] = siteTemplate;
newEntry["Quota"] = quotaTemplate;
newEntry["Status"] = "Pending Approval";
newEntry["SiteFeatureDocID"] = this.SiteFeatureDocID.Checked;
newEntry["SiteFeaturePub"] = this.SiteFeaturesPub.Checked;
newEntry["SiteFeatureActions"] =
  this.SiteFeaturesActions.Checked;
newEntry["SiteFeaturesWebParts"] =
  this.SiteFeaturesWebParts.Checked;
newEntry["WebFeaturesContentOrg"] =
  this.WebFeaturesContentOrg.Checked;
newEntry["WebFeaturesMetaNav"] =
  this.WebFeaturesMetaNav.Checked;
newEntry["WebFeaturesPub"] = this.WebFeaturesPub.Checked;
newEntry["WebFeaturesWikiPage"] =
  this.WebFeaturesWikiPage.Checked;
newEntry.Update();
```

5. We can now close out the top of our `if` block.

6. If the form was not posted then we need to process the form within the `else` block.

```
else
{
  this.SiteCategory.Items.Add("Team Site");
  this.SiteCategory.Items.Add("Project Site");
  this.SiteCategory.Items.Add("Extranet Site");
}
```

7. Once deployed, the rendered version of the **Request Site Collection** page is displayed as follows:

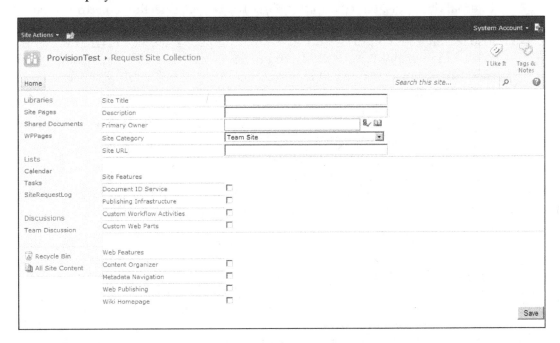

Defining the RequestSiteAction menu item

The request form will need to be easily accessible to all of the site users. One good way to do that is to add it to one of the standard action menus such as the `SiteActions` or `PersonalActions` menu. It will direct the user to the request form wherever they are in the system allowing them to submit the request.

To define a custom action:

1. Click on **Add | New Item** to the Visual Studio project.

2. Under the **SharePoint | 2010** category, select the **Empty Element** type and provide a name such as `RequestSiteAction`.

3. Edit the `Elements.xml` file with the following content:

```
<CustomAction Description="Submit a site collection
  request."GroupId="SiteActions"
  Id="RequestSiteAction"
  Location=
```

```
"Microsoft.SharePoint.StandardMenu"
RequireSiteAdministrator="false" Sequence="1001"
Title="Request Site Collection">
 <UrlAction
  Url="_layouts/SPBlueprintsSiteCreation/RequestSite.aspx" />
</CustomAction>
```

4. When deployed the custom action will be displayed in the **Site Actions** menu, based on the sequence order. With the value of `1001` set, it is displayed at the bottom of the list of actions as shown in the following screenshot:

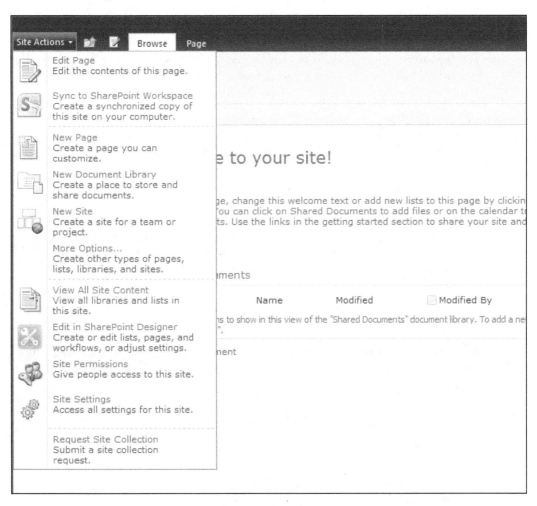

Creating timer jobs

The actual provisioning and configuration of the new site collection will be handled via a timer job instead of making it part of the standard workflow. The provisioning process can be a long running job, and there can be stability problems if too many requests are executed simultaneously. The workflow actions were not intended to support long running jobs such as this. By moving the process to a timer job we can take advantage of the robust scheduling mechanism to queue up the requests, and then handle all of the open requests.

Timer jobs have two main components:

- The class file that holds the actual execution logic that runs when the timer job is active
- The feature receiver is used to handle the initial setup and registration of the job. It will schedule the timer job to run as well as execute any tear down activities that need to happen when the timer job is deactivated

Creating the site timer job

To create the timer job:

1. We will start by adding an **Empty Element** to the solution.
2. We will name the element `CreateSiteTimerJob`.
3. Within the `CreateSiteTimerJob` element we now add a class named `CreateSite`. This class is where the actual timer job and execution logic will reside. We will need to import the following namespaces to support our work:

   ```
   using Microsoft.SharePoint;
   using Microsoft.SharePoint.Administration;
   ```

4. Next, we need to inherit from the `SPJobDefinition` class, which will allow us to perform the timer job functions shown as follows:

   ```
   class CreateSite : SPJobDefinition
   {
     public CreateSite()
       : base() {
     }

     public CreateSite (string jobName, SPService service,
      SPServer server, SPJobLockType targetType)
       : base (jobName, service, server, targetType) {
     }
   ```

```
public CreateSite (string jobName,
 SPWebApplication webApplication)
   : base(jobName, webApplication, null, SPJobLockType.Job)
{
  this.Title = "Create Site";
}
```

Executing the site timer job

The main processing is handled by the override of the `Execute()` method as explained the following steps:

1. The `Execute()` method passes in the `targetInstanceId`, and also provides access to contextual information that we will use to instantiate an `SPWebApplication` object shown as follows:

```
public override void Execute(Guid targetInstanceId)
{
  base.Execute(targetInstanceId);
  SPWebApplication webApp = this.Parent asSPWebApplication;
```

2. We will now request a collection of the pending site requests. To do that, we need to connect to the site that holds the request list. We will load the site specified in the web application's property bag and the SiteRequestSite property.

```
using (SPSite requestSite =
 newSPSite(webApp.Properties["SiteRequestSite"].ToString()))
{
```

3. Next we will define our list query.

```
SPQuery requestQuery = newSPQuery();
requestQuery.Query = "<Where><Eq><FieldRef Name='Status' />
 <Value Type='Choice'>Pending Creation</Value>
 </Eq></Where>";
```

4. Now we are ready to get the item collection by executing the query against the specified list. The list is identified by another property stored in the web application's property bag in a property named `SiteRequestList` shown as follows:

```
SPListItemCollection items =
requestSite.RootWeb.Lists[webApp.Properties["SiteRequestList"].
ToString()].GetItems(requestQuery);
```

5. As it is possible that we have multiple requests pending, we will need to loop through the collection of requests returned from the list, and wrap the code within a `foreach` loop block shown as follows:

```
foreach (SPItem item in items)
{

}
```

6. Before we can create the new site collection, we will need to ensure that a site collection does not already exist at the given address. To do this, we will load the requested path and attempt to connect to the site and web to see if it already exists. If it does not exist, the site will be created.

```
string path = item["Path"].ToString() +
item["URLName"].ToString();
bool siteExists = false;
SPSite tmpSite = null;
try
{
  tmpSite = webApp.Sites["/" + path];
  siteExists = tmpSite.RootWeb.Exists;
}
catch
{
  siteExists = false;
}
finally
{
  if (tmpSite != null)
  {
    tmpSite.Dispose();
  }
}

if (!siteExists){
// Create Site Code
}
else
{
// Update Status of Site Request
  item["Status"] = "Creation Failed";
  item["CreationNotes"] = "URL is not unique.";
  item.Update();
}
```

7. In order to create the site, we will need to identify the site owners' information. To do that we will need to grab the value from the request list and convert it to an `SPUser` object. The following code will handle the conversion:

```
SPFieldUserValue userField =
 new SPFieldUserValue(requestSite.RootWeb,
 item["PriOwner"].ToString());
SPUser priOwner = userField.User;
```

8. Creating the site is done by calling the `Sites.Add()` method and setting the required initial properties such as the `URL`, `Title`, `Description`, `Language`, `Template`, and `Owner` information. There are multiple overrides available and you can choose the one that makes the most sense for your solution. The following is an example of the call included in the sample code. You will notice the `LookupTemplate()` method, which is addressed later in the section.

```
SPSite newSite = webApp.Sites.Add(path,
 item["Title"].ToString(),
 item["Description"].ToString(),
 1033,
 LookupTemplate(item["Template"].ToString()),
 priOwner.LoginName,
 priOwner.Name,
 priOwner.Email);
```

9. We will now set some of the site's properties. These could either be standardized based on your governance policy, or options that are read from the form. All of these properties are properties of the `SPSite` object.

10. In the case of the quota template, it will be important to ensure that the quota templates match what you have registered in the system. The following are the sample properties configured on our sites during the process:

```
newSite.PortalName = "Main Site";
newSite.PortalUrl = "http://Intranet";
newSite.AllowDesigner = true;
if (item["Quota"].ToString() != null)
{
  newSite.Quota =
  SPWebService.ContentService.QuotaTemplates[item["Quota"].
   ToString()];
}
```

11. One of the advantages with automating the site provisioning process is automating the feature activation for common features. In this case there are a number of standard site and web features included on the request form. You can promote the use of certain features by including them on the request form and building them into the site creation process.

12. The feature activation code for the site and the web work the same way, the only difference is where the collection resides. We will start by setting a reference to the `SPFeatureCollection`.

13. Next, we will check our request item to see if the given feature needs to be activated; if so, we will call the `Add()` method with a reference to the feature's GUID, and a Boolean value to force the activation. The following is an example for the Document ID service:

```
SPFeatureCollection siteFeatures = newSite.Features;
if (Convert.ToBoolean(item["SiteFeatureDocID"].ToString()) ==
  true)
    siteFeatures.Add(newGuid("b50e3104-6812-424f-a011-
      cc90e6327318"), true);
```

14. Next, we will update the status of the request list item. This will ensure that it does not get picked up by future jobs, and will also log the date that the site was created for compliance purposes.

```
// update status of site request
item["Status"] = "Complete";
item["CreateDate"] = System.DateTime.Now;
item.Update();
```

15. Make sure SharePoint objects are disposed to avoid memory leaks. Additional details can be found on the MSDN website at: `http://msdn.microsoft.com/en-us/library/ee557362(v=office.14).aspx`

```
newSite.Dispose();
```

16. To update the timer job's progress indicator there is a simple method call that includes a number representing the current percentage.

```
this.UpdateProgress(50);
```

17. The `newSite.Add()` function call included a call to the `LookupTemplate()` function detailed as follows. The purpose of this simple method is to get the internal template value based on the given display name that the requestor specified. The simple `switch` statement can be expanded to include any other site definitions added to the system.

```
private string LookupTemplate(string TemplateName)
{
  string tempID;
  switch (TemplateName) {
    case "Team Site":
      tempID = "STS#0";
      break;
    case "Blank Site":
      tempID = "STS#1";
      break;
    case "Document Workspace":
      tempID = "STS#2";
      break;
    case "Basic Meeting Workspace":
      tempID = "MPS#0";
      break;
    case "Blank Meeting Workspace":
      tempID = "MPS#1";
      break;
    case "Decision Meeting Workspace":
      tempID = "MPS#2";
      break;
    case "Social Meeting Workspace":
      tempID = "MPS#3";
      break;
    case "Multipage Meeting Workspace":
      tempID = "MPS#4";
      break;
    case "Blog":
      tempID = "BLOG#1";
      break;
    case "Wiki":
      tempID = "WIKI#0";
      break;
    default:
      tempID = "STS#0";
      break;
    }
  return tempID;
}
```

Feature receiver

Feature receivers can be used to run code during the feature events including:

- Activation
- Deactivation
- Installed
- Upgrade

This allows for advanced setup and automation capabilities. For the site provisioning feature, we will need to use the feature receiver to manage the status of the site request.

Creating the feature receiver

To create the feature receiver:

1. From the **Solution Explorer**, right-click on `SiteCreationProcess.feature` and select the **Add Event Receiver** option.

2. This will add a class file named `SiteCreationProcess.EventReceiver.cs`. Within this class file you will find some example feature override methods that can be used to handle standard feature events.

3. We need to establish a constant that can be used to support our project shown as follows:

   ```
   conststring TIMER_JOB_NAME = "CreateSite";
   ```

Feature activating

The `FeatureActivated()` method will run whenever the feature is activated, and for our purpose it will be used to register the new timer job:

1. We will uncomment the `FeatureActivated()` method and add the code that is needed to support the feature. As we are scoped for the web application, we will need to grab the context, which we will do with the following line:

   ```
   SPWebApplication webApp = properties.Feature.Parent as
    SPWebApplication;
   ```

2. Now we will run a little code to ensure that a job with the same name is not already registered. If it is, it will be removed.

   ```
   foreach (SPJobDefinition job in webApp.JobDefinitions) {
     if (job.Name == TIMER_JOB_NAME)
       job.Delete();
   }
   ```

3. As our timer job needs to read from the request list, we need a place to store those settings. They could be stored in `web.config`, in an XML file stored somewhere, but the method of choice is to use the web application's property bag, which is easier to maintain than either of the previously identified methods. Before creating the properties we need to do a basic check to see if they already exist. If they do, we will skip the step, if not, then we will create the new properties. At the end we need to be sure to call the `Update()` method so that any changes are saved. This call can add time to your overall processing, so you will want to call it only if changes were made, which we will track using the Boolean variable `isDirty` that we have defined.

```
bool isDirty = false;
if (!webApp.Properties.ContainsKey("SiteRequestList"))
{
  webApp.Properties.Add("SiteRequestList", "SiteRequestLog");
  isDirty = true;
}
if (!webApp.Properties.ContainsKey("SiteRequestSite"))
{
  webApp.Properties.Add("SiteRequestSite",
    "http://intranet/sites/provision");
  isDirty = true;
}
if (isDirty)
  webApp.Update();
```

4. Register the job with a simple reference to the timer job's class file.

```
CreateSiteTimerJob.CreateSite createSite = new
  CreateSiteTimerJob.CreateSite(TIMER_JOB_NAME, webApp);
```

5. Now we need to establish the schedule for the job. There are different scheduling profiles and options including **Minutes**, **Hourly**, **Daily**, **Weekly**, and **Monthly**. As we need this job to run frequently throughout the day, we are going to use the **Minutes** schedule supported by the `SPMinuteSchedule` class. We will set the profile to run every 15 minutes shown as follows:

```
SPMinuteSchedule schedule = newSPMinuteSchedule();
schedule.BeginSecond = 0;
schedule.EndSecond = 59;
schedule.Interval = 15;
createSite.Schedule = schedule;
createSite.Update();
```

Feature deactivating

The `FeatureDeactivating()` method will run whenever the feature is deactivated. Its primary function in this case is to ensure that the timer job is properly moved when the feature is deactivated.

Uncomment the `FeatureDeactivating()` method. The code is the same as what we put in place during activation in case a prior version of the job already existed, but we also need one here so that it can be properly removed if the feature is no longer needed.

```
SPWebApplication webApp = properties.Feature.Parent
as SPWebApplication;

foreach (SPJobDefinition job in webApp.JobDefinitions)
{
  if (job.Name == TIMER_JOB_NAME)
    job.Delete();
}
```

Completed SPBlueprints.SiteCreation solution

The completed **Solution Explorer** for the `SPBlueprints.SiteCreation` solution should look like the following screenshot:

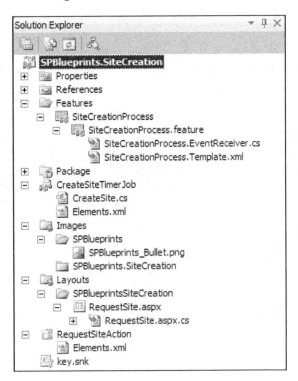

The completed feature should look like the following screenshot:

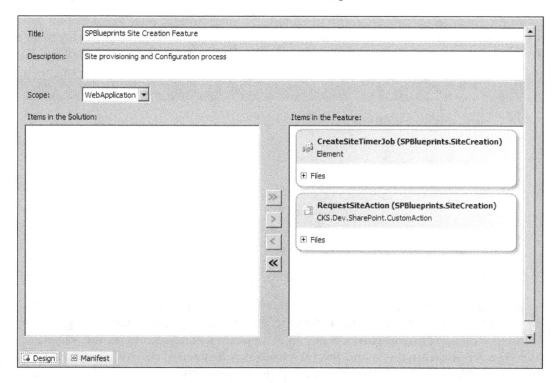

Deploying the timer job

The next step is to compile the solution and deploy the feature to your farm. Before the timer job can properly run, you will just need to set the web application's property bag value for the property named `SiteRequestSite`. This should be set to the path to the site where the request list is stored. With proper configuration in place your job is ready to go.

Monitoring the timer job

With the timer job deployed you will want to be familiar with how to check on it and its status. Within **Central Administration**, under the **Monitoring** section is an area for managing the registered **Timer Jobs** as shown in the following screenshot:

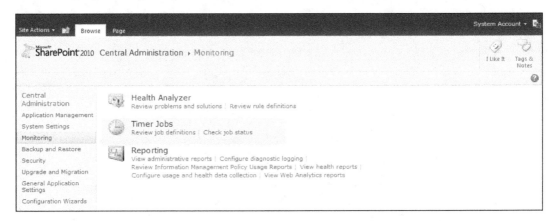

The **Review job definitions** link will list out all of the registered jobs. There are a lot of jobs registered so it is often helpful to filter the list. As the **Create Site** job is defined with a **WebApplication** scope, it is typically a good idea to set the **View** to the **Web Application** view, and then the **Web Application** to the web application you are working with, as shown in the following screenshot:

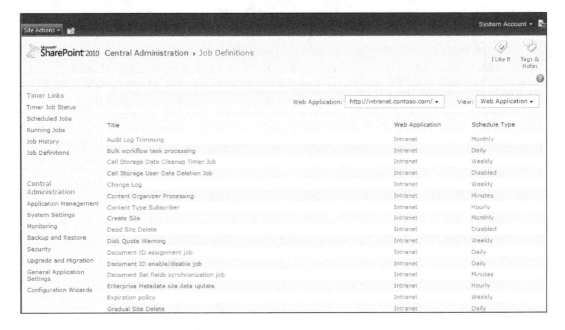

If you click on the title of a registered job, you can view or change its schedule or even run it immediately if desired. A view of the screen is shown as follows:

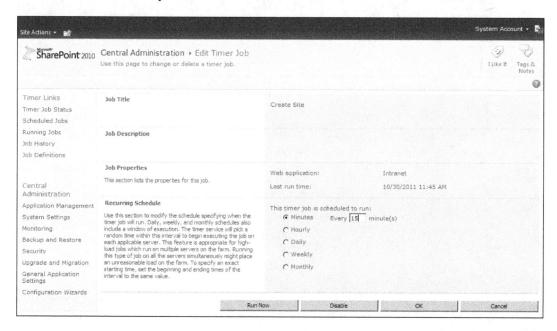

To view the results of a completed job, you can click on the **Job History** link in the upper left-hand side, within **Central Administration**, under the **Job Definitions** section. This will detail out the status of all of the current jobs. Just like with the job definition list, it is possible to filter this down to the web application, making it easier to find your job. Clicking on the **Status** link for a given job will provide a view of the job's execution details including when it ran, how long it ran, and any error messages if applicable.

A view of the **Job History** screen is shown as follows:

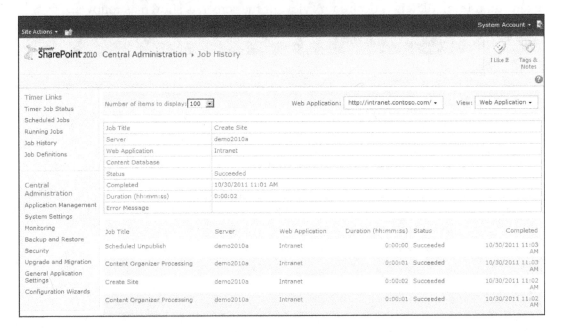

Summary

This chapter leveraged the Server OMs to create packaged solutions in order to deliver the site request and provisioning solution.

The customizations are grouped as follows:

- **Timer job**: A timer job that is used to provision new sites based on requests in a central SharePoint list

- **Feature receiver**: Feature receivers are used to add and remove the timer job registration

- **Application page**: A custom form available globally to request a new site collection

- **Custom action**: Add a menu item to the **Site Actions** menu that links to the site request form, giving users the ability to easily request a new site collection

This chapter showed how you can leverage custom solutions to help automate tedious site administration duties while enhancing governance and compliance capabilities. As these features require a lot of interaction with the farm as a whole, they are not appropriate for sandboxed solutions and would be a challenge to create for the cloud.

6
Building a Project
Site Template

When we think about collaboration sites there are a few types of sites that are commonly used; one of the most common types would be for project-based collaboration. It is easy to start to see very similar content and configuration needs across all sites of this type. Information such as project status, open issues, current project tasks, and project documents are needed throughout all of these sites.

To make it easy to set up and maintain the sites, it is important to come up with a method for creating a site template that can support the site over time. This requires picking a site template approach that can be updated over time, both for new sites being provisioned, as well as applying updates to existing sites.

Overview

This chapter will provide an overview of templating techniques that can be employed to build a robust and maintainable site solution.

The following solution will be created:

- Project site template
- Project web configuration
  - Create a project blog subsite
  - Provision a list through code based on a syndicated content type
  - Create a page library

- ° Create a new homepage
- ° Configure Web Parts on the homepage

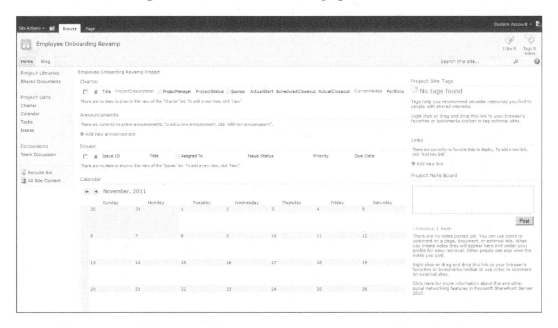

Template options

There are four main options for creating a site template that can be used to create a new site or subsite. They include site definitions, feature stapling an existing site definition, exporting site templates via the UI, and custom code. Each of these options has its own benefits and limitations.

Site definitions

A **site definition** is the root definition of a site and its features in XML. When a site is created, a site definition is referenced, it will always have that dependency, and it cannot be changed easily. The base SharePoint templates including blank, team site, blog site, and so on are all defined as site definitions.

In the earliest versions of SharePoint it was very common, and even recommended, for you to define your own site definitions by creating a feature and including a custom `onet.xml`. The problem with this approach is the dependency that it creates and the difficulty involved with upgrading or migrating that site to another farm or during version upgrades. The dependency has to be maintained and deployed to any of those other farms. During a major platform upgrade, such as SharePoint 2007 to 2010, this can complicate the upgrading process. While not impossible to upgrade, it is difficult, and this approach is now widely discouraged. The alternatives that follow each offer better flexibility without the long-term dependency issues.

Feature stapling an existing site definition

Feature stapling was introduced with SharePoint 2007 and allows you to associate a custom solution with an existing site definition. When that site definition is used, your custom solution will also be executed allowing your changes to be made. This can include adding in custom features like lists, removing lists you do not want to use, or configuring Web Parts. The good news is that the standard site definition is registered, and no changes are made to the standard site definitions.

This is still a valid and supported option with SharePoint 2010, but does not offer all of the flexibility offered in the new `WebTemplates` method described later.

Site template

In previous versions of SharePoint, site owners had the ability to export a site to create a template within the UI. The **Site template** that was created was in the form of an STP file which had some limitations. With SharePoint 2010 the export site template was rewritten to produce a WSP, the standard solution package administrators recognize. The exported solution is added to the Solution Gallery within the Site Collection, essentially making it a Sandbox solution by default.

Developers can take the WSP and import it into Visual Studio if desired using the Import SharePoint Solution Package project type. This will bring the template into Visual Studio 2010 allowing further modifications if needed.

It should not take long to realize that the solution that is exported is bloated and includes definitions for everything including every content type and site column even if they are not being used. If you are going to take this approach it will take significant clean up and refactoring of the project to get it into a maintainable state.

One interesting note about this process is that it relies on the WebTemplates approach that we will review next. The export process basically handles the definition of the `WebTemplate` package, in a single project with multiple solutions.

WebTemplate

The WebTemplates option that was added with SharePoint 2010 attempts to address the core issues with the other solutions.

First, it addresses the issues associated with the site definitions by providing a way to provide a custom `onet.xml` definition, without having to register the custom site definition. It allows you to take a copy of one of the existing `onet.xml` files and make the necessary modifications. The `elements.xml` then references the new `WebTemplate` schema, which is used to define your WebTemplate, and associate it with an existing site definition. While the approach sounds similar to a custom site definition, the important difference is that the site that is provisioned will be identified as using the base site definition referenced. This means that there will be no issue migrating or upgrading the site because of the site definition dependency.

Example WebTemplate schema

Following is a copy of a sample schema with all possible properties:

```
<Elements xmlns="http://schemas.microsoft.com/sharepoint/">
<WebTemplate
AdjustHijriDays="0"
AlternateCssUrl=""
AlternateHeader=""
BaseTemplateID="1"
BaseTemplateName="STS"
BaseConfigurationID="0"
CalendarType="1"
Collation="25"
ContainsDefaultLists="TRUE"
CustomizedCssFiles=""
CustomJSUrl=""
Description="A Custom Team Site."
ExcludeFromOfflineClient="FALSE"
Locale="1033"
Name="TeamPlus"
ParserEnabled="TRUE"
PortalName=""
PortalUrl=""
PresenceEnabled="TRUE"
ProductVersion="4"
QuickLaunchEnabled="TRUE"
Subweb="TRUE"
SyndicationEnabled="TRUE"
Time24="FALSE"
```

```
TimeZone="13"
Title="Custom Team Site"
TreeViewEnabled="FALSE"
UIVersionConfigurationEnabled="FALSE" />
</Elements>
```

The following properties are required, the rest are optional:

Required Property	Notes
BaseTemplateID	Referenced Template ID
BaseTemplateName	Referenced Template Name
BaseConfigurationID	Referenced Configuration ID
Name	Internal Name of your WebTemplate, cannot contain spaces

Sandbox versus farm solutions

The WebTemplate solution can be packaged and deployed as either a Sandbox or Farm solution. How you intend to use the template may dictate which option is better.

Here are some considerations:

- **On Premise SharePoint or Office 365**: Since farm solutions are not supported in Office 365, the sandbox represents the only option
- **Frequently Used Templates**: If the template will be frequently used, it will be quicker and easier to deploy and maintain as a farm solution, because the solution will be maintained centrally instead on each site collection

WebTemplate as a sandbox solution

For the Sandbox solution, the solution should be scoped as for web deployment. The site owner will need to upload the package to the site collection's solution gallery before it can be activated and used. If you are working with a site collection and want to use the solution for subsites then it will be readily available.

A site administrator will need to add the solution to every solution gallery in which it is needed individually, which is the normal pattern with Sandbox solutions, but may get cumbersome for site owners who manage a lot of different site collections.

It is possible to provision new site collections with a `WebTemplate` deployed as a `Sandbox` solution, but it will require some additional steps. When the initial site collection is provisioned, the custom template option should be selected so that the template is identified later. After the core site collection is provisioned, the solution will need to be uploaded to the Solution Gallery.

WebTemplate as a farm solution

In order to get the `WebTemplate` available globally for both new site collections as well as subsites, the solution should be set to deploy as a farm solution with the solution scoped for the farm. This will ensure that it is activated globally and that the template will show up as available within the template catalog for provisioning via central administration, via code, or as a subsite within a site collection.

Organizing a project into multiple features and solutions

A simple site template can be easily configured within a single project and a single solution. Since the `onet.xml` offers the ability to activate other features it is possible to organize your code into multiple features or even solutions. Breaking up your customization into multiple features and solutions will improve the overall maintainability to better support advanced scenarios.

For example, the `WebTemplate` could be included in one solution and then a set of additional features can be included in separate solutions that are activated as part of the overall setup process. If those additional features need to be updated the solutions can be upgraded independently of the `WebTemplate`. In cases like site configuration, properties can be managed and reset this way, Web Parts can be added or moved on pages, or a document library's properties can be modified. The Project Site Template solution developed in this chapter will follow through on this example to illustrate a complex set of solutions.

The following screenshot will present the most common scenario with a set of site and web features identified within the `onet.xml`:

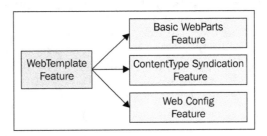

In more advanced scenarios, you may need to activate additional features from within one of your custom features. This would most likely be done within a feature receiver. This type of more complex scenario is illustrated as follows:

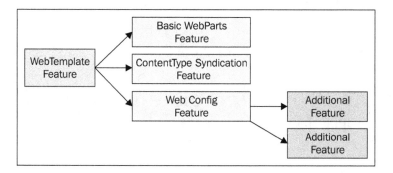

In the scenario for this chapter we will be walking through the creation of a single web template and a feature to configure the template after it is provisioned. If we needed to build a robust library of templates, then there would likely be a single feature that holds all of the web templates, scoped for the farm, and then one feature specific to each template, and perhaps a set of utility features each called from two or more of the other features.

Building the Project Site Template

The Project Site Template will be added to a new project named SPBlueprints. WebTemplates. This project can contain multiple templates as well as any site configuration solutions.

Create the project

To create the initial project:

1. Open Visual Studio 2010.
2. Select **File**, then **New Project**.
3. Browse the installed templates and select **Visual C# | SharePoint 2010**, and then **Empty SharePoint Project**.
4. Enter the project details such as **Name**, **Location**, and **Solution name**.

5. Within the SharePoint Customization Wizard, provide a path to your SharePoint site and then be sure to select the option to **Deploy** as a farm solution.

6. Right-click on the project file and select **Add** then **New Item**.

7. From the template selection screen select the **Empty Element** option

8. Provide the name **ProjectTemplate** and click on the **Add** button.

Create the ProjectTemplate WebTemplate

A web template SPI includes two main artifacts; the Elements.xml and the Onet.xml files.

Complete Elements.xml

As previously described, the Elements.xml will define the web template and associate it with the base site definition. For the ProjectTemplate we will associate this with a standard Team Site. Ensure that the Name property matches the name of your SPI, and that it does not contain any spaces or you will not be able to activate the solution. We will also set the portal site connection which will allow the project sites to lead back to the main project site which we will build out in the next chapter.

```
<WebTemplate
BaseConfigurationID ="0"
BaseTemplateID ="1"
BaseTemplateName ="STS"
Description="A SPBlueprints Project site."
DisplayCategory="SPBlueprints"
Name="ProjectTemplate"
Title="Project Template"
PortalName="Projects Home"
PortalUrl="http://intranet/PMO">
</WebTemplate>
```

Onet.xml

The Onet.xml file is the file used within site definition to define all aspects of the site including navigation, lists, pages, and features:

1. To create a Onet.xml file for your project, copy the onet.xml file for the site definition you want to associate with the web template. You can find the standard site definitions on the SharePoint server in the C:\Program Files\Common Files\Microsoft Shared\Web Server Extensions\14\ TEMPLATE\SiteTemplates directory. Since we referenced the Team Site template, we need to grab the file in the sts\xml\directory.

2. Remove the Modules node block. We only need to include a subset of the content to support the web template feature, and the Modules block is not required or supported.

3. Ensure that there are no FileDialogPostProcess, ExternalSecurityProvider, or ServerEmailFooter elements; if they exist then they must also be removed.

4. Within the Configurations node block, we need to remove all but the configuration ID=0 node block. The Team Site definition supports multiple configurations, but we only want the first node.

5. We then need to ensure that there are no Modules node blocks within the configuration node block.

We now have a good checkpoint for a clean Team Site definition that can be used for all of your web templates. Now we can begin making the changes used to support our specific template.

The next thing we want to do is configure the NavBars block which controls the Quick launch and Top link bar navigation items.

To customize the navigation:

1. The NavBar element exists in the standard onet.xml, but there is no link present so we will add a NavBarLink element.

```
<NavBar Name="$Resources:core,category_Top;" Separator="&amp;nbs
p;  " Body="&lt;a ID='onettopnavbar#LABEL_ID#'
href='#URL#' accesskey='J'&gt;#LABEL#&lt;/a&gt;" ID="1002" >
<NavBarPage Name="Home" Url="" />
</NavBar>
```

2. Add a `NavBar` element for the `Project Libraries` item header shown as follows:

```
<NavBar Name="Project Libraries" Url="_layouts/viewlsts.
aspx?BaseType=1" ID="1004" />
```

3. Add a `NavBar` element for the `Project Lists` item header shown as follows:

```
<NavBar Name="Project Lists" Url="_layouts/viewlsts.
aspx?BaseType=0" ID="1003" />
```

4. Add a `NavBar` element for the `Discussions` item header shown as follows:

```
<NavBar Name="Discussions" Url="_layouts/viewlsts.aspx?BaseType=0&
amp;ListTemplate=108" ID="1006" />
```

The next thing we want to do is add to any standard lists to the site.

To add an instance to a standard list:

1. For any standard list templates, we can add the following definition to the Lists node block.

```
<List FeatureId="00bfea71-5932-4f9c-ad71-1557e5751100"
Type="1100"
Title="Issues"
Url="$Resources:core,lists_Folder;/Issues"
QuickLaunchUrl="$Resources:core,lists_Folder;/Issues/AllItems.
aspx"
/>
```

2. Next, we will add any site scoped features we wish to activate.

```
<SiteFeatures>
<!-- BasicWebParts Feature -->
<Feature ID="00BFEA71-1C5E-4A24-B310-BA51C3EB7A57" />
<!-- Three-state Workflow Feature -->
<Feature ID="FDE5D850-671E-4143-950A-87B473922DC7" />
<!-- Doc ID Service Feature -->
<Feature ID="b50e3104-6812-424f-a011-cc90e6327318" />
<!-- Content Type Syndication -->
<Feature ID="73EF14B1-13A9-416b-A9B5-ECECA2B0604C" />
<!-- Ent Site Features -->
<Feature ID="8581a8a7-cf16-4770-ac54-260265ddb0b2" />
<!-- Std Featurs -->
<Feature ID="b21b090c-c796-4b0f-ac0f-7ef1659c20ae" />
</SiteFeatures>
```

3. Finally, we will add any web scoped features we wish to activate.

```
<WebFeatures>
<!-- TeamCollab Feature -->
<Feature ID="00BFEA71-4EA5-48D4-A4AD-7EA5C011ABE5" />
<!-- MobilityRedirect -->
<Feature ID="F41CC668-37E5-4743-B4A8-74D1DB3FD8A4" />
<!-- SPBlueprints Web Config -->
<Feature ID="3b3eb230-2649-4ace-996f-ed6e97494a04" />
</WebFeatures>
```

Once the `Onet.xml` files are complete, we need to change the file's Deployment type property to ElementsFile so that it can be properly deployed.

The last WebFeature in the list `SPBlueprints Web Config` is a reference to a second feature we will now add to the solution. Ensure that the GUID matches the corresponding GUID to your new feature.

Configure the feature

We will now configure the main solution that will contain the web templates. This solution will be scoped for a farm deployment so that it is available for provisioning site collections in a single step, without the need to upload or activate the template. This would also make it available for the automated site provisioning process previously reviewed.

To configure the ProjectTemplate-Farm feature:

1. Rename **Feature 1** to `ProjectTemplate-Farm`.
2. Change the **Title** to `Project Site Template`.
3. Change the **Description** to `SPBlueprints Project Site Template`.
4. Change the **Scope** to `Farm`.

The completed feature is displayed as follows:

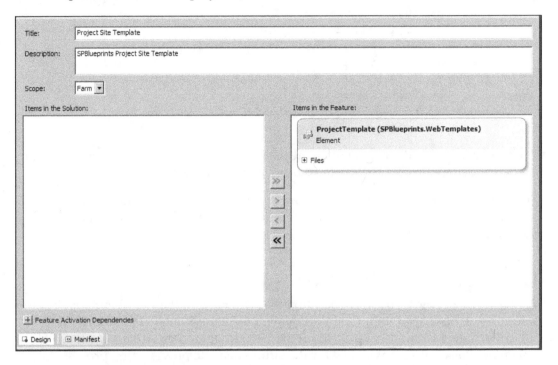

Create the Project Site configuration feature

As discussed in the WebTemplate overview section at the beginning of the chapter, it is possible to call custom features from within the WebTemplates definition. Organizing your work into multiple features will help to provide additional capabilities to execute code for configuration items that either cannot be set declaratively in the CAML within the onet.xml file or need to be handled later in the overall execution chain.

There is also the added benefit that the solution can be maintained over time through feature versioning and upgrading. When a new version is deployed it would be possible to execute the updates allowing for any needed changes to be automatically deployed or configured.

We will define an additional feature at this time, a feature that will not contain any SPIs, but will have a feature receiver that executes to make any required modifications.

To configure the ProjectWebConfig-Web feature:

1. Right-click on the **Features** node and select **Add Feature**.
2. Rename **Feature 1** to `ProjectWebConfig-Web`.
3. Change the **Title** to `Project Web Configuration`.
4. Change the **Description** to `SPBlueprints Project Web Configuration - Hidden Feature`.
5. Change the **Scope** to `Web`.
6. Change the **Is Hidden property** to `true`.
7. Right-click on the **ProjectWebConfig-Web** feature and select **Add Event Receiver**.

The completed feature is displayed in the following screenshot:

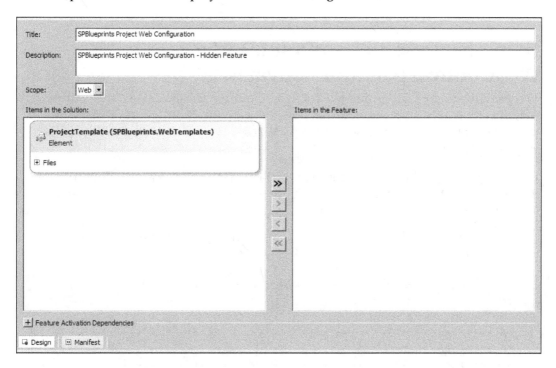

Writing the feature receiver

The feature receiver can support multiple event methods to cover the different feature lifecycle events such as `FeatureActivated`, `FeatureDeactivating`, and `FeatureUpgrading`. These events are what will assist us in maintaining the sites over time.

The first step is to establish the required references to support our work. We will import the following namespaces:

```
using System;
using System.Runtime.InteropServices;
using System.Security.Permissions;
using System.IO;
using System.Xml;
using System.Web.UI;
using Microsoft.SharePoint;
using Microsoft.SharePoint.Administration;
using Microsoft.SharePoint.Navigation;
using Microsoft.SharePoint.Security;
using Microsoft.SharePoint.Utilities;
using Microsoft.SharePoint.WebPartPages;
using Microsoft.SharePoint.WebControls;
```

Using Microsoft.SharePoint.Portal. WebControls;Feature Activated

The `FeatureActivated()` method is the method that is called when the feature is activated, and it is the method that will make the final configuration changes to the site at the time it is provisioned, since this feature is activated as part of the WebTemplate code.

We will start by grabbing a reference to the SPWeb from the feature properties and then wrap the rest of the code within a `try/catch` block to ensure any exceptions are trapped and logged to the ULS logs.

```
public override void FeatureActivated(SPFeatureReceiverProperties
properties)
{
SPWeb web = (SPWeb)properties.Feature.Parent;
try
{
// **********************************************************
// Main Code Here
// **********************************************************
}
catch (Exception ex)
    {
SPSecurity.RunWithElevatedPrivileges(delegate()
```

```
        {
// Log to ULS Log
        SPDiagnosticsService.Local.WriteTrace(0, new
SPDiagnosticsCategory("SP Blueprints Site Configuration",
TraceSeverity.Unexpected, EventSeverity.Error), TraceSeverity.
Unexpected, ex.Message, ex.StackTrace);
        });
}
}
```

Within the main try block we will create code blocks that perform the desired configuration changes. These steps represent examples of changes that can be automated as part of the site creation process.

The following functions will be included:

- **Create a blog subsite**: A subsite for the project site for communicating project news
- **Create the charter list**: A list that contains project charter information
- **Create the pages library**: A library that will contain our Web Part pages
- **Create the homepage**: A Web Part page added to the Pages library
- **Configure Web Parts on the homepage**: We will add the desired Web Parts and list view Web Parts to the homepage

Create a blog subsite

The first thing we will do within the main code block is to provision a blog subsite. This will give the project team a way to communicate out to the project's stakeholders and participants.

When creating a site, it is important to check to see if the site already exists so we will do a simple check prior to creating the site. If this is the first time this code is run, the site should not exist, but if the feature were to be deactivated and reactivated on an existing site, this code will run an additional time.

```
SPWeb blog = web.Webs["Project Blog"];
if (!blog.Exists) {
blog = web.Webs.Add("blog", "Project Blog", "Blog for project
communications.", 1033, SPWebTemplate.WebTemplateBLOG, false, false);
```

With the blog site created, we now want to make sure that it is set to inherit the main project site's navigation and then add it to the main project site's top navigation. Calling the Update() method will save the changes.

```
blog.Navigation.TopNavigationBar.Navigation.UseShared = true;
blog.Update();
SPNavigationNode blogNode = new SPNavigationNode("Blog", blog.
ServerRelativeUrl);
web.Navigation.TopNavigationBar.AddAsLast(blogNode);
web.Navigation.GlobalNodes.AddAsLast(blogNode);
web.Update();
```

Now we need to close out our if block and dispose our SPWeb object. For additional guidance on best practices for disposing SharePoint objects see: http://msdn.microsoft.com/en-us/library/ee557362(v=office.14).aspx

Create Charter list

In previous chapters we created a number of content types, list definitions, and list instances declaratively in our solutions. An alternative is to create those lists using the object model. Creating them with the object model can provide some advantages in maintainability, but it is also a necessity in cases where you want to establish a list from an existing content type. In this case, the ProjectCharter content type is syndicated via the Content Type hub.

The first thing we want to do is check to see if the list exists.

```
bool listExists = false;
try{
SPList temp = web.Lists["Charter"];
listExists = true;
}
catch{
listExists = false;
}
```

If the list does not exist, we will create the list.

```
if (!listExists) {
Guid guidCharter = web.Lists.Add("Charter", "Project Charter",
SPListTemplateType.GenericList);
SPList listCharter = web.Lists[guidCharter];
listCharter.OnQuickLaunch = true;
```

Then add the ProjectCharter content type to the list.

```
listCharter.ContentTypes.Add(web.AvailableContentTypes
["ProjectCharter"]);
listCharter.Update();
```

Now we will want to modify the default view to add in the `ProjectCharter` fields.

```
SPView defaultView = listCharter.Views[0];
defaultView.ViewFields.Add("ProjectDescription");
defaultView.ViewFields.Add("ProjectManager");
defaultView.ViewFields.Add("ProjectStatus");
defaultView.ViewFields.Add("Sponsor");
defaultView.ViewFields.Add("ActualStart");
defaultView.ViewFields.Add("ScheduledCloseout");
defaultView.ViewFields.Add("ActualCloseout");
defaultView.ViewFields.Add("CurrentNotes");
defaultView.ViewFields.Add("Portfolio");
defaultView.Update();
```

Create pages library

We will now create a document library that can be used to store the Web Part pages including our home page. Before we attempt to create the library, we will want to check to see if it already exists.

```
bool libExists = false;
string libName = "Pages";

foreach (SPList list in web.Lists){
if (list.Title == "Pages"){
libExists = true;
    break;
}
}
```

If the library does not exist, we will add one to the current web.

```
if (!libExists) {
web.Lists.Add(libName, "Content Pages", SPListTemplateType.
DocumentLibrary);
}
```

Create home page

Next we will create a new page in the previously created pages library and configure it to hold the desired Web Parts.

There are a number of different page types including:

- **Basic home page**: The basic Web Part page template typically employed by a team site. It includes Web Part zones and the Quick launch menu on the left hand side.

- **Web Part pages**: A Web Part page template that includes Web Part zones in various configurations, but does not include a Quick launch menu.

- **Publishing pages**: A Web Part page template available when the publishing infrastructure is activated. They support the selection of a page layout and support page level metadata attributes.

- **Wiki Pages**: Wiki Pages are the default page types for a Wiki.

The Wiki Pages make it difficult to programmatically configure them since the Web Part zones are dynamically generated and therefore difficult to reference, so they are not a great option if you are adding and customizing Web Parts on the page.

First we will get a reference to the Pages library we previously created and establish some other working variables. The `newFilename` variable is the name of the page we want to create and the `templateFilename` is the name of the template we are using. The `GetGenericSetupPath` points to a template file in the main SharePoint root.

```
SPFolder libFolder = web.GetFolder(libName);
string newFilename = "Home.aspx";
string templateFilename = "default.aspx";
string path = SPUtility.GetGenericSetupPath("TEMPLATE\\SITETEMPLATES\\
STS\\");
SPFile newFile = null;
```

Next we will check to see if the page already exists, and if it exists we will delete it so that it can be recreated with the current configuration.

```
foreach (SPFile page in libFolder.Files) {
if (page.Name == newFilename) {
libFolder.Files["Home.aspx"].Delete();
libFolder.Update();
break;
}
}
```

We can now create the page. We will read the template file referenced into a `FileStream` object into a new file created within the folder object we have a reference to. Be sure to close and dispose the `FileStream` object, or the process will put a lock on your template file, which will prevent any additional processes from using it.

```
FileStream stream = new FileStream(path + templateFilename, FileMode.
Open);
SPFileCollection files = libFolder.Files;
newFile = files.Add(newFilename, stream);
stream.Close();
stream.Dispose();
```

We now need to set the new page as the `WelcomePage` for the web's `RootFolder` which will ensure that any user going to the root of the web will be directed to this page instead of getting a Page Cannot Be Found error.

```
web.AllowUnsafeUpdates = true;
SPFolder rootFolder = web.RootFolder;
rootFolder.WelcomePage = newFile.Url;
rootFolder.Update();
web.AllowUnsafeUpdates = false;
```

Configure Web Parts on home page

We now have a reference to the page and can add the desired Web Parts to the page. Adding Web Parts to the page is done through the `SPLimitedWebPartManager` object. We can get a reference to the object within our new file for the given `PersonalizationScope`; in this case the Shared scope.

```
SPLimitedWebPartManager wpMgr = newFile.
GetLimitedWebPartManager(System.Web.UI.WebControls.WebParts.
PersonalizationScope.Shared);
```

The first Web Part we will add to the page is the Tag Cloud Web Part, which will be configured to show the tags for all users for the content within this site and all of its subsites. The Tag Cloud Web Part has a number of configuration properties that will be set including the `ShowCount` which determines if the number of items tagged should be included and `UserScope` which is what determines which tags to show, in this case the tags for all users from this site.

When we add the reference to the Web Part to the `SPLimitedWebPartManager` object, we also need to define the Web Part zone to use and a position reference.

```
TagCloudWebPart tagWebPart = new TagCloudWebPart();
tagWebPart.Title = "Project Site Tags";
```

```
tagWebPart.ShowCount = true;
tagWebPart.UserScope = TagCloudUserScope.UnderUrlEveryone;
wpMgr.AddWebPart(tagWebPart, "Right", 2);
wpMgr.SaveChanges(tagWebPart);
```

Next we will add a Note Board Web Part to the page so that stakeholders can leave comments on the page or ask questions. The `WebPartPropertyDisplayItems` will determine the number of items to show before paging starts.

```
SocialCommentWebPart noteboardWebPart = new SocialCommentWebPart();
noteboardWebPart.Title = "Project Note Board";
noteboardWebPart.WebPartPropertyDisplayItems = 10;
wpMgr.AddWebPart(noteboardWebPart, "Right", 3);
wpMgr.SaveChanges(noteboardWebPart);
```

Next we will add a `ListViewWebPart` to the page which is a Web Part representation of one of the site's lists or libraries. We will start by adding a Web Part for the Charter list that was created. Since we will be adding multiple `ListViewWebParts` to the page, I have created a utility function named `ConfigureWebPart` to assist with the common steps. This method will be detailed later.

We will pass the `ConfigureWebPart` method a reference to the `SPList` object, the name of the zone, and a Boolean value, to determine if the default view should be used, and we get a populated Web Part object in return. We will pass that Web Part object to the `SPLimitedWebPartManager` and save the changes.

```
ListViewWebPart charterWebPart = ConfigWebPart(web.Lists["Charter"],
"Left", true);
wpMgr.AddWebPart(charterWebPart, charterWebPart.ZoneID, 1);
wpMgr.SaveChanges(charterWebPart);

Similar to the Charter ListViewWebPart, we will now add the Issues,
Calendar and Links lists to the page.

ListViewWebPart issuesWebPart = ConfigWebPart(web.Lists["Issues"],
"Left", true);
wpMgr.AddWebPart(issuesWebPart, issuesWebPart.ZoneID, 3);
wpMgr.SaveChanges(issuesWebPart);
ListViewWebPart calendarWebPart = ConfigWebPart(web.Lists["Calendar"],
"Left", false);
wpMgr.AddWebPart(calendarWebPart, calendarWebPart.ZoneID, 4);
wpMgr.SaveChanges(calendarWebPart);
ListViewWebPart linksWebPart = ConfigWebPart(web.Lists["Links"],
"Right", false);
wpMgr.AddWebPart(linksWebPart, linksWebPart.ZoneID, 1);
wpMgr.SaveChanges(linksWebPart);
```

For the announcements list we will want to configure that one a little more explicitly so it will not use the ConfigWebPart() method and instead make all of the changes inline. We will establish a reference to the SPList object, create the ListViewWebPart and then set the desired properties before adding it to the SPLimitedWebPartManager.

```
SPList announ = web.Lists["Announcements"];
ListViewWebPart announcementsWebPart = new ListViewWebPart();
announcementsWebPart = new ListViewWebPart();
announcementsWebPart.Title = announ.Title;
announcementsWebPart.ZoneID = "Left";
announcementsWebPart.ListName = announ.ID.ToString("B").ToUpper();
announcementsWebPart.TitleUrl = announ.DefaultViewUrl;
pMgr.AddWebPart(announcementsWebPart, announcementsWebPart.ZoneID, 2);
wpMgr.SaveChanges(announcementsWebPart);
wpMgr.Dispose();
```

We need to ensure that the SPLimited WebPartManager object is properly disposed when we are done with it to prevent memory leaks.

While completing the code that configured the ListViewWebParts we referenced a utility function called ConfigWebPart that helped to set some standard configuration for the Web Parts properties. The method is provided with a reference to the SPList, the zone to place the Web Part, and a Boolean value to determine if the default view should be used. In the case of most regular lists, the default view and its fields should be applied, but in cases where there are special styles applied to the ListViewWebPart views, the default view should not be applied. Examples include the Links and Announcement lists which have different visual formatting by default. At the end, the configure Web Part object is returned.

```
private ListViewWebPart ConfigWebPart(SPList list, string zoneID, bool
setDefaultView)
{
ListViewWebPart wp = new ListViewWebPart();
wp = new ListViewWebPart();
wp.Title = list.Title;
wp.ZoneID = zoneID;
wp.ListName = list.ID.ToString("B").ToUpper();
wp.TitleUrl = list.DefaultViewUrl;
    if (setDefaultView)
            wp.ViewGuid = list.DefaultView.ID.ToString("B").ToUpper();
return wp;
}
```

Feature upgrading

SharePoint 2010 has added some new capabilities to better support the lifecycle of your custom solutions. With proper versioning and adoption of the feature upgrade patterns, it is possible to add additional Web Parts to the page, define additional lists, add or modify list columns, and so on. This functionality is critical to maintaining a solution like this Project Site template solution which is likely to be used on dozens of sites, but also needs the changes available for any new sites that are provisioned. Since the upgrades can be applied to specific version ranges, it is possible to support the features in multiple previously controlled states.

Solution Explorer

The completed **Solution Explorer** is shown in the following screenshot:

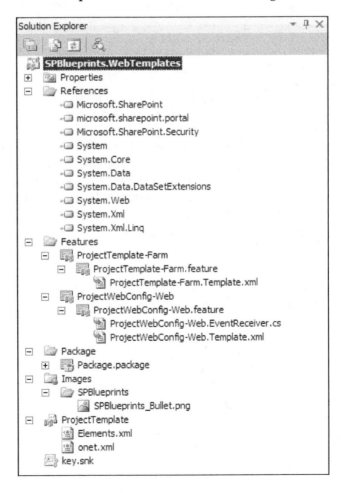

Summary

This chapter leveraged the Server OMs and a series of packaged features in order to deliver the Project Site Template solution.

The customizations are grouped as follows:

Visual Studio 2010

- **WebTemplate**: To create a `WebTemplate` feature that defines a site template and activates the desired features.
- **Feature receiver**: To create a feature receiver that handles additional web provisioning, creates required lists and libraries, and then creates and configures a home page with the desired Web Parts.

This chapter showed how you can use the `WebTemplates` feature to build robust custom site templates that are maintainable. Also, by moving the additional configuration code to a separate solution we provided a way that we can maintain our sites over time allowing for changes and reconfiguration of existing sites as needed.

In the next chapter, *Building a Project Management Office Site*, we will leverage the content from these sites to create a master rollup site which will give people the ability to view summary data across all related sites.

7
Building a Project Management Main Site

In the previous chapter we went through the steps to design a reusable web template that can be used to provision a site to support a standard business process. The example we used was for project management, but it could have also been used for numerous other examples including product management, process improvement, inventory management, and so on. The value of creating those sites with standard templates and definitions is twofold; it cuts down on the amount of configuration needed when setting up each site, but it also provides a standardized set of content that can be aggregated and displayed on top-level sites.

This chapter takes us through the development of a Project Management Master site that can aggregate the key metrics and status information from the project management sites previously created. In addition, the site can also include process and community content similar to what was originally covered in *Chapter 4, Building an Engaging Community Site*.

This chapter covers the following topics:

- Project listing and status Web Part
- Rollup metrics
- My Project Sites listing
- Project Manager listing

By the end of this chapter we will be able to create a site capable of aggregating content and information from a number of project subsites.

Content aggregation options

As the content is organized across many site collections, it is important that the process used to get the information executes very quickly and efficiently. Depending on the type of content you are aggregating and how it will be used, the type of approach may change. In this case the content will also be somewhat dynamic with new project sites being provisioned on a regular basis. It would be impossible to maintain a manual list of all of the active projects.

There are three main approaches that can be considered: reading for the individual sites, using search, and compiling information via a scheduled job.

Reading individual sites or lists

The simplest way to read data from the Server OM is to make a call to `SPList.GetItems` for a given list. While this works great when you know exactly what you are looking for, and from which specific locations, it does not tend to be a great way to aggregate content, because it is too specific and does not scale as well as some of the other approaches.

It is also possible to query for all of the content within a site collection by making a call to `SPWeb.GetSiteData`. This is significantly more flexible than the previous method because it casts a wider net and looks throughout the site collection, but it would still require iterating through each site collection and would require that you know which site collections contain the content you are looking for.

Using these methods should not be the primary aggregation method, but can be combined with one of the following, to query additional content or details.

Search

The search index provides a great way to quickly and efficiently access content from a wide range of sources, especially when aggregating a list of similar or related content from a wide range of sites. It is possible to use `KeywordQuery`, `FullTextSQLQuery`, or in cases where FAST is available, FQL queries.

To increase the accuracy and speed of the queries, it is possible to fine-tune the query and configuration to target-specific search scopes, content types, and managed properties. Specifying the search scope will shrink the number of source records you are searching against, and specifying a content type or a managed property will allow you to filter the results down to a very precise level.

The first challenge to using the search index is that your content needs to be indexed regularly for accurate results in cases where your content changes frequently. In most cases incremental crawls are sufficient to pick up any new or modified content. If your content changes more frequently than it can be crawled, you may need to use an alternative approach.

The second challenge to using the search index is that very specific queries that filter or return content based on custom properties will need to have managed properties established, in order for the indexing process to recognize the specific fields and values. Setting up managed properties for a handful of specified fields is not a big deal, but mapping a dozen or more fields for a single solution might be cumbersome. An alternative to this approach would be to execute a simplified query to quickly get a list of content sources, and then iterate through that list and execute a call to the `SPList.GetItems` or `SPWeb.GetSiteData` method that was outlined earlier.

Scheduled job

In cases where you need to aggregate content for more complicated purposes, such as for a scorecard on a dashboard, it is not advisable to gather the data in real-time. In these cases it is advisable to run a timer job to generate the results. This will simplify the process by providing a single source for pulling the summary data or aggregated content.

Map custom properties as managed properties

As we saw in the *Search* section earlier, it is necessary to create managed properties for individual fields that we will return or filter by within our search query.

To create the mapping:

1. Navigate to the **Search Service Application**.
2. Click on the **Metadata Properties** link under the **Queries and Results** heading.
3. Provide a **Property name**, **Value**, and a **Description**.
4. Under the **Mappings to crawled properties** section, click on the **Add Mapping** button and search for the field identified in the content type.
5. Select the appropriate mapping and click on the **OK** button.

This will need to be completed for the following properties:

- `Portfolio`
- `ProjectDescription`
- `ProjectManager`
- `ProjectStatus`
- `Sponsor`
- `ScheduledStart`
- `ActualStart`
- `ScheduledCloseout`
- `ActualCloseout`
- `ProjectHealth`

Building a project listing and a status Web Part

As part of the Project Site Template created in the previous chapter, there is a simple list based on a syndicated content type called `ProjectCharter` that provided some information about the project. While it is set as a regular list, there would only be a single record per site. This information is a great example of the type of information that can be rolled up into a central listing. This listing will be created with the `ProjectListing` Web Part which leverages the Server OM and search to dynamically find all of the indexed projects. In addition, the projects' current project status records can also be displayed from the central listing, which provides a convenient way to review the information.

Creating the ProjectMain project

The `ProjectListing` Web Part will be added to a new project called `SPBlueprints.ProjectMain`.

To create the initial project:

1. Open Visual Studio 2010.
2. Select **File**, then **New Project**.
3. Browse to the **Installed Templates** and select **Visual C# | SharePoint 2010**, and then **Empty SharePoint Project**.
4. Enter the project details such as **Name**, **Location**, and **Solution name**.

5. Within the **SharePoint Customization Wizard**, provide a path to your SharePoint site and then be sure to select the option to **Deploy as a farm solution**.

Creating the ProjectListing Web Part

To create the Web Part:

1. Right-click on the project file and select **Add New Item**.

2. From the template selection screen select the **Web Part** option.

3. Provide the name `ProjectListing` and click on the **Add** button.

4. Edit the `ProjectListing.webpart` file.

5. Set the **Title** property to `ProjectListing`.

6. Set the **Description** property to `SPBlueprints Project Listings`.

7. Create a property named `SearchProxyName` and set it to the name of your Search service application.

8. Create a property named `SearchScopeName` and set it to `Project Sites`.

9. Create a property named `DisplayLimit` and set it to `50`.

10. Edit the `ProjectListing.cs` file.

11. Import the following namespaces to support our work:

```
using System;
using System.Collections;
using System.ComponentModel;
using System.Data;
using System.Text;
using System.Web;
using System.Web.UI;
using System.Web.UI.WebControls;
using System.Web.UI.WebControls.WebParts;
using Microsoft.SharePoint;
using Microsoft.SharePoint.WebControls;
using Microsoft.SharePoint.Administration;
using Microsoft.Office.Server.Search;
using Microsoft.Office.Server.Search.Query;
using Microsoft.Office.Server.Search.Administration;
```

12. The following variables should be defined to support the Web Part:

```
private string searchProxyName;
private string searchScopeName;
private int displayLimit;
```

```
protected Literal _output;
protected Label labelStatus;
protected DropDownList choiceStatus;
protected Label labelSort;
protected DropDownList choiceSort;
```

13. Next we need to override the `CreateChildControls()` method and instantiate each of the ASP.NET controls.

```
protected override void CreateChildControls()
{
  this.labelStatus = newLabel();
  this.labelStatus.ID = "labelStatus";
  this.labelStatus.Text = "Status:       ";
  this.Controls.Add(this.labelStatus);

  this.choiceStatus = newDropDownList();
  this.choiceStatus.ID = "choiceStatus";
  this.choiceStatus.Items.Add("Active");
  this.choiceStatus.Items.Add("All");
  this.choiceStatus.Items.Add("Identified");
  this.choiceStatus.Items.Add("Scheduled");
  this.choiceStatus.Items.Add("In Progress");
  this.choiceStatus.Items.Add("Closeout");
  this.choiceStatus.Items.Add("Complete");
  this.choiceStatus.AutoPostBack = true;
  this.Controls.Add(this.choiceStatus);

  this._output = newLiteral();
  this._output.ID = "output";
  this.Controls.Add(this._output);
}
```

14. The following Web Part properties should be defined to allow settings to be configured instead of hard-coding them into the Web Part code:

```
#region WebPart Properties
[WebBrowsable(true),
Category("Project Listing Properties"),
WebDisplayName("Search Proxy Name"),
WebDescription("Please provide the name of your Search Service
 Application."),
Personalizable(PersonalizationScope.Shared)]
public string SearchProxyName
{
  get { return searchProxyName; }
```

```
    set { searchProxyName = value; }
  }


  [WebBrowsable(true),
  Category("Project Listing Properties"),
  WebDisplayName("Search Scope Name"),
  WebDescription("Please provide the name of your Search
    Scope."),
  Personalizable(PersonalizationScope.Shared)]
  public string SearchScopeName
  {
    get { return searchScopeName; }
    set { searchScopeName = value; }
  }


   [WebBrowsable(true),
  Category("Project Listing Properties"),
  WebDisplayName("Result limit"),
  WebDescription("The number of items to display."),
  Personalizable(PersonalizationScope.Shared)]
  public int DisplayLimit
  {
    get { return displayLimit; }
    set { displayLimit = value; }
  }
  #endregion
```

15. The output will be created in the `Display()` method, which should be called as a part of the `OnLoad()` method. The overall output will be maintained within the `messages` StringBuilder object.

```
protectedvoid Display()
{
  this.EnsureChildControls();
  StringBuilder messages = newStringBuilder();
```

16. As we will be using SharePoint Search to help surface the content, we will need to test a connection to the Search service application specified in the Web Part properties. If the connection cannot be established, then the error should be caught and handled within the `catch` block.

```
try
{
  SearchQueryAndSiteSettingsServiceProxy settingsProxy =
   SPFarm.Local.ServiceProxies.GetValue
   <SearchQueryAndSiteSettingsServiceProxy>();
```

```
SearchServiceApplicationProxy searchProxy =
 settingsProxy.ApplicationProxies.GetValue
 <SearchServiceApplicationProxy>(this.searchProxyName);
FullTextSqlQuery mQuery = newFullTextSqlQuery(searchProxy);

// Additional Formatting Code
catch
{
  this.EnsureChildControls();
  this._output.Text = "Error: Please specify a Search Service
   Application.";
}
```

17. The remaining code will all reside within a `try`/`catch` block. There is a choice control that provides the user the opportunity to filter down the records to actual status values, as well as some virtual status values that can include one of multiple values.

```
try
{
  string filter = "Active";
  if (this.choiceStatus.SelectedValue != null)
    filter = this.choiceStatus.SelectedValue;

  ResultTableCollection resultsTableCollection;
  DataTable results = newDataTable();
  bool bAltRow = true;
```

18. The query will identify the specific managed properties we want to display, the scope to select it from, and the filter that will be used. It is important to remember that the managed properties have to be mapped in order to be used in the queries, so only fields mapped to a managed property can be used. To help increase accuracy and further improve performance, we can reference the Project Sites scope instead of the All Sites scope, in order to apply an additional set of filtering rules. We are looking specifically for records within the ProjectCharter content type so that needs to be added to the WHERE clause of the query.

```
mQuery.QueryText = "SELECT Portfolio, Title,
 ProjectDescription, ProjectManager, ProjectStatus, Sponsor,
 ScheduledStart, ActualStart, LastModifiedTime, Path, SiteName,
 ScheduledCloseout, ActualCloseout  FROM SCOPE()
 WHERE (\"scope\" = 'Project Sites') AND
 Contains(ContentType,'ProjectCharter') ";
```

19. To help support the status filtering we will use a `switch` block that can support showing multiple statuses related to the `"Active"` status, show records from all statuses, or from a specific status that might be selected. This could be extended to show other logical groupings similar to the `"Active"` status if needed.

```
switch (filter)
{
  case "Active":
    mQuery.QueryText += "AND (ProjectStatus = 'Identified' OR
     ProjectStatus = 'Scheduled' OR ProjectStatus =
     'In Progress')";
    break;
  case "All":
    break;
  default:
    mQuery.QueryText += "AND ProjectStatus = '" + filter + "'";
    break;
}
```

20. Next we can set the remaining query properties, execute the query, and check to see if the results were returned.

```
mQuery.ResultTypes = ResultType.RelevantResults;
mQuery.TrimDuplicates = true;
mQuery.RowLimit = DisplayLimit;
resultsTableCollection = mQuery.Execute();

if (resultsTableCollection.Count > 0){
```

21. Next we will extract just the relevant results from the returned `ResultTableCollection` object.

```
ResultTable relevantResults =
 resultsTableCollection[ResultType.RelevantResults];
results.Load(relevantResults, LoadOption.OverwriteChanges);
```

22. Next we will reference a JavaScript file that will contain client-side code to support the status pop-up display.

```
messages.Append("<script type='text/ecmascript'
 src='/_layouts/SPBlueprints.ProjectMain/ProjectMain.js'>
 </script>");
```

23. The display could be done using `SPGridView`, but in order to have complete control over the display, we can format the output as a simple HTML table. This is defined in the following code snippet, along with the header row, to define the fields that will be displayed. In order to adopt the standard SharePoint styles, we will reference the CSS classes used by a standard `SPGridView`.

```
messages.AppendFormat(@"<table width='100%' border='0'
 cellpadding='1' cellspacing='0' class='ms-listviewtable'>
 <tr class='ms-viewheadertr ms-vhltr'><th class=
 'ms-vh2'>Portfolio</th><th class='ms-vh2'>Title</th>
 <th class='ms-vh2'>Project Description</th><th class=
 'ms-vh2'>Project Manager</th><th class='ms-vh2'>Status</th>
 <th class='ms-vh2'>Sponsor</th><th class='ms-vh2'>Scheduled
 Start</th><th class='ms-vh2'>Actual Start</th><th class=
 'ms-vh2'>Scheduled End</th><th class='ms-vh2'>Last
 Modified</th></tr>");
```

24. To provide the row output we will now use a simple `foreach` loop, which can iterate through the available rows. In order to provide a link to the project site and to the status listing within the pop up, we will also need to execute some string manipulation on the `sitePath` value that was returned from the search results.

```
foreach (DataRow row in results.Rows)
{
  string sitePath = row[10].ToString();
  sitePath = sitePath.Substring(0, sitePath.Length - 13);
  string statusPath = String.Concat(sitePath,
   "Lists/Status/AllItems.aspx?isDlg=1");
```

25. Next we will define the row tags, and include a logic check to see if the alternating row needs to be styled. The remainder of the row is written out including a link to the project site and a call to the `javascript:showStatus()` method, which will load the project's status list view in a Client OM modal dialog window. Afterwards the alternating row flag is changed before closing out the `foreach` loop and then closing the HTML table.

```
messages.AppendFormat(@"<tr ");
if (bAltRow) { messages.AppendFormat(@"class=
 'ms-alternatingstrong'"); }
messages.AppendFormat(@"><td>{0}</td><td>
 <a href='{10}'>{1}</a></td><td>{2}</td><td>{3}</td><td>
 <a href=""javascript:showStatus('{12}','{1}');"">{4}</a>
 </td><td>{5}</td>
```

```
          <td>{6}</td><td>{7}</td><td>{8}</td><td>{9}</td></tr>",
          row[0].ToString(), row[1].ToString(), row[2].ToString(),
          row[3].ToString(),row[4].ToString(), row[5].ToString(),
          String.Format("{0:M/d/yyyy}", row[6]),
          String.Format("{0:M/d/yyyy}", row[7]),
          String.Format("{0:M/d/yyyy}",
          row[11]), row[8].ToString(), row[9].ToString(),
          row[10].ToString(),statusPath);

        bAltRow = !bAltRow;
      }
      messages.AppendFormat(@"</table>");
```

26. Finally we will set the final output, provide the `catch` block to grab and report any errors, and then use the `finally` block to ensure that the query object is properly disposed.

```
      }
      this.EnsureChildControls();
      this._output.Text = messages.ToString();
    }
    catch (Exception ex)
    {
      this.EnsureChildControls();
      this._output.Text = "<br />Error: " + ex.Message.ToString();
    }
    finally
    {
      mQuery.Dispose();
    }
```

Creating the ProjectMain.js script

Our Web Part output includes references to a JavaScript file that is used to display the project's status list view in a Client OM modal dialog window.

To add this script:

1. In **Solution Explorer**, right-click and select **Add**, and select the **SharePoint "Layouts" Mapped Folder** option.

2. Select the project folder.

3. Right-click and select **Add | New Item**.

4. Under the **Web** category select the **Jscript** file option.

5. Name the file `ProjectMain.js`.

6. Click on the Add button.

The ProjectMain.js file will initially contain a single method named showStatus(), which will format and open a Client OM modal dialog window with a reference to the project site's status list.

```
function showStatus(statusUrl, statusTitle) {
  var _options = { url: statusUrl, width: '1200',
   height: '600', title: statusTitle };
  SP.UI.ModalDialog.showModalDialog(_options);
}
```

Configuring the feature

We will now configure the main solution that will contain the Web Parts. This solution will be scoped for a site deployment.

To configure the ProjectMain-Web feature:

1. Rename **Feature 1** to ProjectMain-Web.

2. Change **Title** to Project Main.

3. Change **Description** to SPBlueprints Project Main Site Feature.

4. Change **Scope** to **Site**.

The completed feature is displayed in the following screenshot:

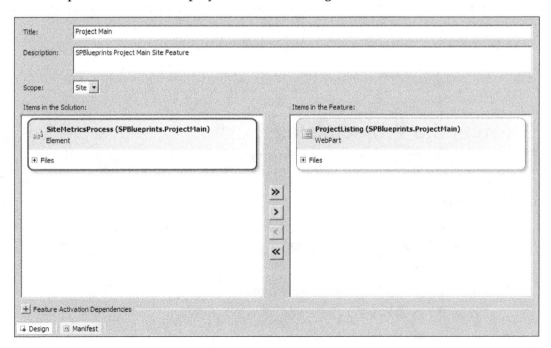

Project listing displayed

The final rendered view is displayed in the following screenshot:

View status for a project is displayed in the following screenshot:

Building a site metrics gathering process

In order to gather the metrics for the active projects we will use a timer job to support the scheduled job scenario reviewed at the beginning of the chapter.

To create the timer job:

1. Start by adding an **Empty Element** to the solution.

2. **Name** the element SiteMetricsProcess.

3. Within the SiteMetricsProcess SPI, we now need to add in a class named SiteMetricsTimerJob.cs. This class is where the actual timer job and its execution logic will reside.

4. We will need to import the following namespaces to support our work:

```
using System;
using System.Collections.Generic;
using System.Data;
```

```
using Microsoft.Office.Server.Search;
using Microsoft.Office.Server.Search.Query;
using Microsoft.Office.Server.Search.Administration;
using Microsoft.SharePoint;
using Microsoft.SharePoint.Administration;
```

5. Next, we need to inherit from the SPJobDefinition class, which will allow us to perform the timer job functions displayed as follows:

```
class SiteMetricsTimerJob : SPJobDefinition
{
  public SiteMetricsTimerJob() : base() {
  }
  public SiteMetricsTimerJob (string jobName,
   SPService service, SPServer server,
   SPJobLockType targetType)
    : base (jobName, service, server, targetType) {
  }
  public SiteMetricsTimerJob(string jobName,
   SPWebApplication webApplication)
    : base(jobName, webApplication, null, SPJobLockType.Job)
  {
    this.Title = "Project Site Metrics Collection";
  }
```

6. The main processing is handled by the override of the Execute method. The Execute method passes in targetInstanceId, and also provides access to the contextual information that we will use to instantiate an SPWebApplication object displayed as follows:

```
public override void Execute(Guid targetInstanceId)
{
  base.Execute(targetInstanceId);
  SPWebApplication webApp = this.Parent as SPWebApplication;
```

7. Next, we will establish a connection with the search proxy, and create a FullTextSQLQuery object, which is very similar to the Web Part we recently created.

```
SearchQueryAndSiteSettingsServiceProxy settingsProxy =
 SPFarm.Local.ServiceProxies.
 GetValue<SearchQueryAndSiteSettings ServiceProxy>();
SearchServiceApplicationProxy searchProxy =
 settingsProxy.ApplicationProxies.
 GetValue<SearchServiceApplicationProxy>
 (webApp.Properties["SearchProxyName"].ToString());
FullTextSqlQuery mQuery = new FullTextSqlQuery(searchProxy);
ResultTableCollection resultsTableCollection;
DataTable results = new DataTable();
```

8. As we are only looking to collect summary metrics, the search query can be simplified to only include a couple of properties needed to generate the metrics.

```
mQuery.QueryText = "SELECT Title, ProjectStatus FROM SCOPE()
WHERE (\"scope\" = 'Project Sites') AND
Contains(ContentType,'ProjectCharter') ";

mQuery.ResultTypes = ResultType.RelevantResults;
mQuery.TrimDuplicates = true;
resultsTableCollection = mQuery.Execute();

if (resultsTableCollection.Count > 0)
{
  ResultTable relevantResults =
   resultsTableCollection[ResultType.RelevantResults];
  results.Load(relevantResults, LoadOption.OverwriteChanges);
```

9. With the results returned and available within a `DataTable` object, we can generate the individual metrics we need. For this, we will call the `Select()` method with an expression to gather the matched records, and then set a local variable for later use.

```
string exp;

// Identified Items
exp = "ProjectStatus = 'Identified'";
DataRow[] matchedIdenRows;
matchedIdenRows = results.Select(exp);
int iIden = matchedIdenRows.GetUpperBound(0) + 1;

// Scheduled Items
exp = "ProjectStatus = 'Scheduled'";
DataRow[] matchedSchedRows;
matchedSchedRows = results.Select(exp);
int iSched = matchedSchedRows.GetUpperBound(0) + 1;

// In Progress Items
exp = "ProjectStatus = 'In Progress'";
DataRow[] matchedInProgRows;
matchedInProgRows = results.Select(exp);
int iInProg = matchedInProgRows.GetUpperBound(0) + 1;

// Closeout Items
exp = "ProjectStatus = 'Closeout'";
DataRow[] matchedCloseoutRows;
matchedCloseoutRows = results.Select(exp);
int iCloseout = matchedCloseoutRows.GetUpperBound(0) + 1;
```

```
// Completed Items
exp = "ProjectStatus = 'Complete'";
DataRow[] matchedCompRows;
matchedCompRows = results.Select(exp);
int iComp = matchedCompRows.GetUpperBound(0) + 1;
```

10. We now have all of the information we need to update the central metrics list. To start with, we will connect to the site specified in the property bag, open the web, and connect to the list specified in the property bag. We will grab the All Items view which will have the five status values, and set each of them to the summary values that were gathered earlier before saving the updates.

```
using (SPSite site = new
 SPSite(webApp.Properties["ProjectSiteMetrix"].ToString()))
{
  using (SPWeb web = site.OpenWeb())
  {
    SPList metrics =
    web.Lists[webApp.Properties["ProjectSiteMetrixList"].
     ToString()];
    SPListItemCollection items =
    metrics.GetItems(metrics.Views["All Items"]);

    SPListItem item;
    item = items[0];
    item["Title"] = "Identified";
    item["Sites"] = iIden;
    item.Update();

    item = items[1];
    item["Title"] = "Scheduled";
    item["Sites"] = iSched;
    item.Update();
    item = items[2];
    item["Title"] = "In Progress";
    item["Sites"] = iInProg;
    item.Update();
    item = items[3];
    item["Title"] = "Closeout";
    item["Sites"] = iCloseout;
    item.Update();

    item = items[4];
    item["Title"] = "Complete";
    item["Sites"] = iComp;
    item.Update();
```

Creating the feature and feature receiver

Another feature will be added to support the timer job, and allow for registering and removing the job during activation and deactivation.

To add the feature:

1. Right-click on the **Features** node and select the **Add Feature** option.
2. Rename the feature `ProjectMain-App`.
3. Provide a **Title** property.
4. Provide a **Description** for the feature.
5. Set the scope of the feature to **WebApplication** to support activation once per web application.

A feature receiver must be created to register the job on activation or remove it, when it is deleted.

To create the feature receiver:

1. From **Solution Explorer**, right-click on `ProjectMain-App.feature` and select the **Add Event Receiver** option. This will add a class file named `ProjectMain-App.EventReceiver.cs`. Within this class you will find some example feature override methods that can be used.
2. The next thing we need to do is establish a constant that can be used to support our project shown as follows:

```
const string TIMER_JOB_NAME = "SiteMetricsProcess";
```

3. Next, we will uncomment the `FeatureActivated()` method and add the code that is needed to support the feature. As we are scoped for the web application, we will need to grab the context which we will do with the following line:

```
SPWebApplication webApp = properties.Feature.Parent as
  SPWebApplication;
```

4. Now we will run a little code to ensure that a job with the same name is not already registered. If it is, it will be removed.

```
foreach (SPJobDefinition job in webApp.JobDefinitions) {
  if (job.Name == TIMER_JOB_NAME)
    job.Delete();
}
```

5. As our timer job needs to read from and write to a SharePoint list, we will use the property bag to maintain those settings. We will check to see if the required keys exist, and create them and set a value if they do not. At the end we need to be sure to call the `Update()` method, so that any changes are saved. This call can add time to your overall processing, so you will want to only call it if changes were made, which we will track using the Boolean variable `isDirty` that we have defined.

```
bool isDirty = false;
if (!webApp.Properties.ContainsKey("SearchProxyName"))
{
  webApp.Properties.Add("SearchProxyName",
   "Search Service Application");
  isDirty = true;
}
if (!webApp.Properties.ContainsKey("SearchScopeName"))
{
  webApp.Properties.Add("SearchScopeName", "Project Sites");
  isDirty = true;
}
if (!webApp.Properties.ContainsKey("ProjectSiteMetrixList"))
{
  webApp.Properties.Add("ProjectSiteMetrixList",
   "ProjectSiteMetrics");
  isDirty = true;
}
if (!webApp.Properties.ContainsKey("ProjectSiteMetrix"))
{
  webApp.Properties.Add("ProjectSiteMetrix",
   "http://intranet/PMO/");
  isDirty = true;
}
if (isDirty)
  webApp.Update();
```

6. Next we will register the job with a simple reference to the timer job's class file and create the schedule. The metrics can be set to generate on a frequency that meets the requirements. In this example we will set it to run once daily, but it could be generated at any frequency needed.

```
SiteMetricsProcess.SiteMetricsTimerJob metricsProcess =
 new SiteMetricsProcess.SiteMetricsTimerJob(TIMER_JOB_NAME,
 webApp);

SPDailySchedule schedule = newSPDailySchedule();
schedule.BeginSecond = 0;
schedule.EndSecond = 59;
metricsProcess.Schedule = schedule;
metricsProcess.Update();
```

7. We also want to make sure that we have proper clean up actions so we will now uncomment the `FeatureDeactivating()` method. The code is the same as what we put in place during activation in case a prior version of the job already existed, but we also need one here so that it can be properly removed if the feature is no longer needed.

```
SPWebApplication webApp = properties.Feature.Parent as
 SPWebApplication;

foreach (SPJobDefinition job in webApp.JobDefinitions)
{
  if (job.Name == TIMER_JOB_NAME)
    job.Delete();
}
```

Solution Explorer

The completed **Solution Explorer** is shown in the following screenshot:

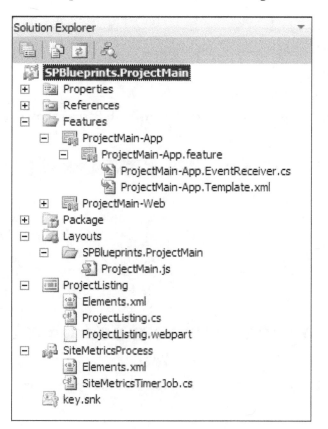

Configuring a project manager listing

The **Project Managers** page will display a listing of all of the people with a title of Project Manager. This will leverage SharePoint's People Search and the People Search Core Results Web Part to execute a set query that looks at the `JobTitle` field.

Creating the members page

To create the members page:

1. Click on the **Site Actions** menu, and select the **New Page** item.

2. Provide a **Title** for the page.

3. Click on the **Create** button.

Adding the People Search Core Results Web Part

To add the People Search Core Results Web Part to the page:

1. Click on the **Insert** tab of the Ribbon.

2. Select the **Web Part** action.

3. Select the **Search** category.

4. Select the **People Search Core Results** Web Part as shown in the following screenshot:

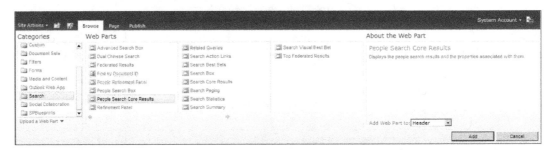

Configuring the members search query

To configure the preset members search query:

1. Edit the **People Search Core Results** Web Part properties.

2. Under the **Display Properties** group, change the **Default Results Sorting** to **Name**.

3. Set the **Results Per Page** value to 50.

4. Uncheck the **Use Location Visualization** checkbox to enable customizing the XSL as shown in the following screenshot:

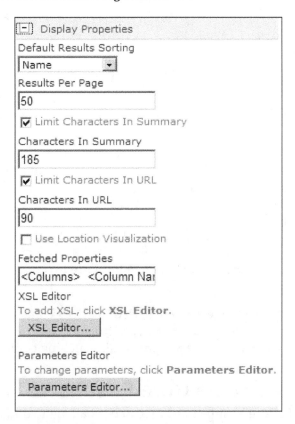

5. Click on the **XSL Editor** button to open the model window with the XSL that formats the results.

6. Make any desired modifications (see the next section).

7. Click on the **Save** button to save your changes.

8. Under the **Results Query Options** group, change the **Cross-Web Part query ID**.

9. Change the **Fixed Keyword Query** to JobTitle:"Project Manager" as shown in the following screenshot:

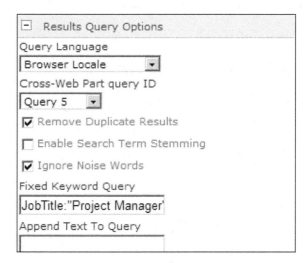

10. Under the **Appearance** group, change the **Title** to Our Project Managers.

11. Click on the **OK** button.

12. The **Fixed Keyword Query** value added in step 9 will do a managed property search for the JobTitle field, looks for matches with the value "Project Manager", and returns all matching contacts.

Modifying the People Core Results XSL

The standard People Core Results markup can be changed to add or remove properties in order to display the desired content. The standard markup is organized into two main div containers: ContactInfo and MoreInfo. The ContactInfo contains properties that are of value, but we will be changing the contents of the MoreInfo container in order to focus on their skills, interests, and previous projects. We will also remove the About Me property, and apply formatting changes.

Within the XSL, search for the `MoreInfo` container. Immediately before the `MoreInfo` container there is a conditional statement that should be removed so that the properties are displayed consistently.

```
<xsl:if test="$hasabme or $hasresp or $hassk or $hasint or
$hasorgparent or $hasmem or $haspp or $hassch or $hasbol or
$hassum">
```

Next we will replace the About Me property with the Past Projects property, which is more meaningful in this context.

Remove the following section:

```
<xsl:if test="$hasabme">
  <li>
    <span id="FieldTitle">
      <xsl:value-of select="$AboutMeLabel" />
    </span>
    <xsl:apply-templates select=
      "hithighlightedproperties/aboutme" />
  </li>
</xsl:if>
```

And replace it with:

```
<li>
  <span id="FieldTitle">
    <xsl:value-of select="$PastProjectsLabel" />
  </span>
  <xsl:call-template name="RenderSimpleMultivalue">
  <xsl:with-param name="multivalue"
   select="hithighlightedproperties/pastprojects"/>
  <xsl:with-param name="cutoff" select="5"/>
  </xsl:call-template>
</li>
```

For the Responsibilities, Skills, and Interests sections, be sure to remove the conditional test that wraps each section. With this conditional test in place, it will only show the section if it was related to the search term.

The remaining properties within this section can be removed.

Project Managers listing displayed

The final rendered view is displayed in the following screenshot:

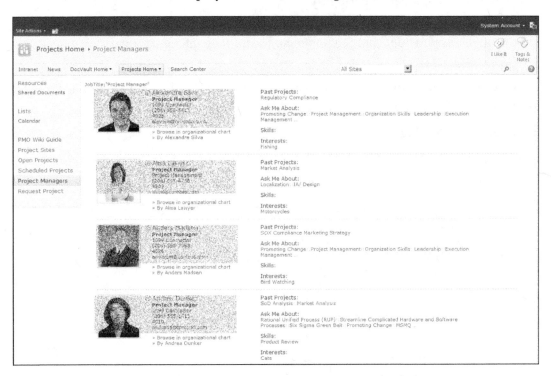

Additional content ideas

With a project main site, it may be desirable to aggregate additional project details like project issues or milestones, which can be done following a similar pattern to what was done with the project charter information.

It may also be desirable to display content recently modified across the sites, or content edited by the current user following a pattern similar to the DocVault Listings Web Part reviewed in *Chapter 3, Building an Enterprise Content Management Solution*.

In addition, the community content and features reviewed in *Chapter 4, Building an Engaging Community Site* may also provide value to your project participants.

Summary

This chapter leveraged both the Server and Client OMs along with some community based libraries to create a packaged solution that can provide a Project Management rollup site.

The customizations are grouped as follows:

- Visual Studio 2010:
    - ○ **Web Part**: Used to display both the main project metrics as well as provide a way to view the detailed project status
    - ○ **Timer job**: Used to update the metrics on a scheduled basis
    - ○ **Feature receiver**: Used to register and unregister the timer job
- Browser based configuration:
    - ○ **Configure People Core Results Web Part**: Configured to pull the listing of project managers along with custom XSL to enhance the format of the results

This chapter showed how you can:

- Aggregate content across site collections using both the search subsystem as well as the regular list APIs to query content
- Mix both the server and client code within the same solution in order to build a highly functional and efficient solution, which is critical when pulling content from potentially hundreds of sites
- Use techniques for generating aggregate metrics that can be processed via a scheduled process, in order to increase the speed for rendering the content on demand

The next chapter will address the business need to aggregate a user's tasks from across the entire system or a selection of sites, providing an effective way to surface the tasks and increase the chances that they will be completed in a timely fashion.

8
Building a Task Rollup Solution

For organizations that are widely using SharePoint to support workflows or task management, it can be important to find an effective way to make those tasks accessible throughout the system, or at least in particular places like the user's MySite or the front page of a portal. As there is no solution included that meets this need, it represents another great example of a custom solution that can be built to extend the platform to provide a critical business solution.

This chapter will provide an overview of the approaches that can be leveraged to aggregate the tasks from multiple sites into a single display, along with the trade-offs of each approach. In addition to the conceptual overview, the following customizations will be created:

- MyTasks Search Web Part
- MyTasks Web Part

Task rollup options

To aggregate the tasks into a single listing there are three options that can be considered:

- Using search to query the content from the index
- Querying the lists directly with `SiteData`
- Running a scheduled process that can create a reference to the task in a centralized list

We will review the advantages and disadvantages of each approach and determine where you would want to use or not use it for your scenario.

Using search

As we have seen in the example solutions throughout the book, search can provide a very effective way to aggregate content from many different sources quickly. The biggest advantage is the speed of retrieving the results, and the fact that it can work with results that have very different attributes and metadata schemas.

Search considerations

One of the risks with using search for this solution is that the accuracy of the displayed results will vary greatly depending on how current the crawl index is. The timeliness or freshness of the record is probably more important with tasks than any other content stored in SharePoint, because tasks can be actively worked throughout the day with new tasks being added, and existing ones being updated or completed. If the index is stale, it will lead to inaccurate information being displayed, which will lead to a lack of trust in the solution.

In order to successfully use search, the crawl schedule will need to be as frequent as possible for the content sources that contain the tasks. Moving towards a continuous, or at least near continuous, crawl will help ensure more accurate results. If crawls cannot be completed frequently enough, then using the search index is not a good idea.

Using SiteData

It is also possible to query the list information within the sites. This provides a good case for using the SPSiteDataQuery class, which provides a mechanism to define a list query across multiple lists simultaneously, either within the scope of the given web or the entire site collection. When used with the GetSiteData() method within the SPWeb object, you can effectively execute a complex query used to aggregate content.

The SPSiteDataQuery object has the following key properties:

Property	Description
Lists	The Lists property is used to specify the Base List Type or List Template associated with the list.
ViewFields	The ViewFields property identifies the fields that should be returned. Adding Nullable = True will ensure that the field is included even if all list items do not include that field in its schema. The ViewFields property format should be a valid CAML.
Query	The Query property identifies any filtering or ordering that should be done to the results. The Query property format should be a valid CAML.
Webs	The Webs property identifies the scope with the two main options being Recursive, which will execute the query against the current site and all subsites, or SiteCollection, which will execute the query against the entire site collection.

The SPWeb.GetSiteData() method can be used to execute the referenced SPSiteDataQuery object and returns a standard DataTable object in response.

SiteData considerations

As we will see later in this chapter, the SiteData option can be very effective when used wisely, but has the potential to cause some serious performance issues if used inappropriately. As the widest scope that it can query is a site collection, you will need to make a call to each site collection you want to check for tasks. If there are only a handful of site collections, this may not be that risky, but if you have dozens of site collections it is sure to perform slowly or with hundreds of sites it will surely fail.

Particular care should be taken when considering how to identify and move through the sites that you will execute the query against. Apart from proper disposal of the SPSite objects, it is also nearly always a good idea to avoid iterating through the entire SPSiteCollection, unless you are certain that the number of site collections is small.

Using a centralized list

It is possible to aggregate the content in a centralized list so that the data can be retrieved quickly. This could be done using either of the following methods:

- An event receiver could be written that automatically copies the reference to each new task or updates any existing task

- A custom timer job could be written that could execute the `GetSiteData()` method on each site collection, and then write the results to the central list

Centralized list considerations

While these approaches may make sense for some solutions and content, I do not believe that either would be a good fit for aggregating task data.

For the event receiver option, event receivers may not be reliable enough to keep the items in sync throughout all task lists within the entire environment, and will add significant overhead to your servers.

The timer job option is not a good idea for two reasons. The first reason for this is that it would have to be done for all users, not just the ones using the customization which will result in wasted processing. The second reason is that this approach will be limited by the same constraint as using the search index; it will only be as accurate as the last collection job. Running the job too frequently will have a large impact on the server, because the timer job is unlikely to have the scalability or parallelism built into the search crawling process.

MyTasks Search Web Part

The MyTasks Search Web Part will utilize the search approach to pull together a listing of all the user's tasks.

Creating the SPBlueprints.MyTasks project

The MyTasks Search Web Part will be added to a new project called `SPBlueprints.MyTasks`.

To create the initial project:

1. Open Visual Studio 2010.
2. Select **File**, then **New Project**.
3. Browse the **Installed Templates** and select **Visual C# | SharePoint 2010**, and then **Empty SharePoint Project**.

4. Enter the project details such as **Name**, **Location**, and **Solution name** as shown in the next screenshot.

5. Within the **SharePoint Customization Wizard**, provide a path to your SharePoint site and then be sure to select the option to **Deploy as a farm solution**.

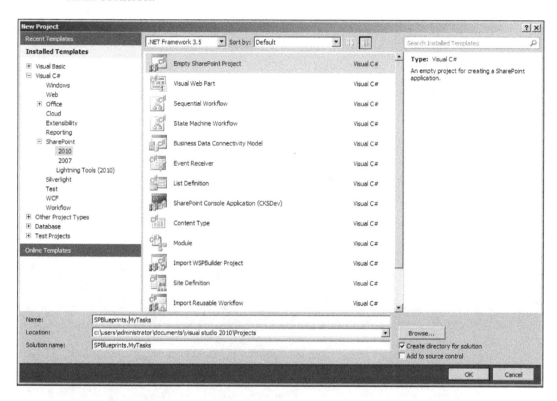

Creating the MyTasks Search Web Part

To add the Web Part to the SPBlueprints.MyTasks project:

1. Open the SPBlueprints.MyTasks project in Visual Studio 2010.

2. Browse the **Installed Templates** and select **Visual C# | SharePoint 2010**.

3. Right-click on the project file and select **Add | New Item**.

4. From the template selection screen select the **Web Part** option.

5. Provide the **Name** as MyTasks Search and click on the **Add** button as shown in the following screenshot:

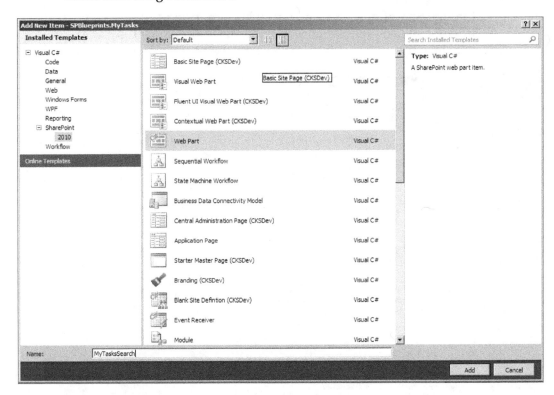

6. Edit the MyTasksSearch.webpart file and add in the custom properties shown as follows:

```
<property name="Title" type="string">MyTasks Search</property>
<property name="Description"type="string">Task Rollup Web
 Part</property>
<property name="DisplayMode"type="string">List</property>
<property name="SearchProxyName"type="string">Search Service
 Application</property>
```

7. The project will need to add references to both the Microsoft.Office. Server and Microsoft.Office.Server.Search DLLs. With those references in place the following namespaces should be imported to your Web Part file:

```
Using System.Data;
Using System.Text;
```

```
Using Microsoft.Office.Server.Search;
Using Microsoft.Office.Server.Search.Query;
Using Microsoft.Office.Server.Search.Administration;
```

8. The Web Part will include a number of properties with configuration settings and the output format of the content. First we will define the Display Mode property which is used to determine the format of the output using a simple enumeration to designate a List or Table format.

```csharp
private displayMode _displayMode;
public enum displayMode
{
  List,
  Table
}

[WebBrowsable(true),
  Category("Configuration"),
  WebDisplayName("Display Mode"),
  WebDescription("Please select the display mode."),
  Personalizable(PersonalizationScope.Shared)]
public displayMode DisplayMode
{
  get { return _displayMode; }
  set { _displayMode = value; }
}
```

9. Next we will define the Search Proxy Name which is used to connect to the Search service application of your choice.

```csharp
private string _searchProxyName;
[WebBrowsable(true),
  Category("Configuration"),
  WebDisplayName("Search Proxy Name"),
  WebDescription("Please provide the name of your Search
    Service Application."),
  Personalizable(PersonalizationScope.Shared)]
public string SearchProxyName
{
  get { return _searchProxyName; }
  set { _searchProxyName = value; }
}
```

10. The output will be built within a `Literal` control defined within the class, and instantiated within the `CreateChildControls()` method shown as follows:

```
protected Literal _output;
protected override void CreateChildControls()
{
  this._output = newLiteral();
  this._output.ID = "output";
  this.Controls.Add(this._output);
}
```

11. The `LoadTasks()` method will be used to get any relevant task information in the search index. To start out we will identify an initial `DataTable` to hold our results, and then establish a connection to the Search service application specified in the Web Part's properties. This is encapsulated within a `try`/`catch` block in order to capture any exceptions connecting to the service application.

```
private DataTable LoadTasks()
{
  DataTable results = new DataTable();
  try
    {
      SearchQueryAndSiteSettingsServiceProxy settingsProxy =
       SPFarm.Local.ServiceProxies.
       GetValue<SearchQueryAndSiteSettingsServiceProxy>();
      SearchServiceApplicationProxy searchProxy =
       settingsProxy.ApplicationProxies.
       GetValue<SearchServiceApplicationProxy>
       (this._searchProxyName);
      FullTextSqlQuery mQuery =
       new FullTextSqlQuery(searchProxy);

// Remaining code here
    }
  catch
  {
    this.EnsureChildControls();
    this._output.Text = "Error: Please specify a Search Service
     Application.";
  }
  return results;
}
```

12. As long as the connection with the service application was successful, the remaining code will execute. For proper exception handling, the remaining code will be enclosed in another `try/catch/finally` block to support displaying any unexpected exceptions, and to properly dispose the query object.

13. We will start by getting the current user's information, and then formatting the `FullTextSQLQuery` syntax to return the information we are looking for. We identify the properties that need to be returned.

 The properties must be set up as Managed Metadata Properties in the Search service application to be selectable.

```
try
{
  string user =
   SPContext.Current.Web.CurrentUser.Name.ToString();
  ResultTableCollection resultsTableCollection;
  mQuery.QueryText = "SELECT Title, Path, AssignedTo, Status, "
   + " WorkflowName, StartDate, EndDate"
   + " FROM SCOPE() WHERE (\"scope\" = 'All Sites')"
   + " AND ContentClass='STS_ListItem_Tasks'";
  mQuery.ResultTypes = ResultType.RelevantResults;
  mQuery.TrimDuplicates = false;
  mQuery.RowLimit = 100;
```

14. We can now execute the query and set the results in the `resultsTableCollectionDataTable` object. We will then check to see if there are any items, and if so, pull out the items identified as relevant results and load those in the results `DataTable` object.

```
resultsTableCollection = mQuery.Execute();
if (resultsTableCollection.Count> 0)
{
  ResultTable relevantResults =
   resultsTableCollection[ResultType.RelevantResults];
  results.Load(relevantResults, LoadOption.OverwriteChanges);
}
```

15. We can now close out the `try` block and add the `catch` block to trap any exceptions and include the exception message in the Web Part's output.

```
}
catch (Exception ex)
{
  this.EnsureChildControls();
```

```
this._output.Text+= ex.Message;
}
  finally
{
  mQuery.Dispose();
}
```

16. The `Display()` method will be used to define the Web Part's output and will be called from the `OnLoad()` method. The method starts by defining the `StringBuilder` object we will use to build the output of the Web Part, and then calls the `LoadTasks()` method we just defined to load the actual data. We can then start to format the output of our content and register the `MyTasks.js` script.

```
protected void Display()
{
  StringBuilder messages = new StringBuilder();
  try
  {
    DataTable results = LoadTasks();
    messages.AppendFormat(@"<br>My Tasks: {0}",
      results.Rows.Count);
    messages.AppendFormat(@"<div id='MyTasks'><ul>");
    messages.AppendFormat(@"<script type='text/ecmascript'
      src='/_layouts/SPBlueprints.MyTasks/MyTasks.js'>
      </script>");
```

17. We will use a `switch` block to control the multiple versions of the output which supports both a `List` and `Table` version. If the value of the Display Mode Web Part property is `List`, the first case will be met and the content will be shown in a simple list format.

18. A `foreach` loop will then be used to iterate through each row in the included results `DataTable` object. Within the loop we will handle some conditional formatting for the `WorkflowName` field, and display it within brackets if there is a value. Then we will write out the list item tag for the given task, close the list and close the `div` container object before breaking the `case` statement.

```
switch (_displayMode)
{
  case displayMode.List:
  foreach (DataRow row in results.Rows)
  {
    string workflow = "";
      if (row[4].ToString() != "")
        workflow = "(" + row["WorkflowName"].
```

```
      ToString() + ")";
      messages.AppendFormat(@"<li>
      <a href=""javascript:showTask('{0}', '{1}',
      '{2}')"">{1}</a> {2}</li>", row[1].ToString(),
      row[0].ToString(), workflow);
    }
  messages.AppendFormat(@"</ul></div>");
  break;
```

19. The second case supports the Display Mode of `Table` which will render an HTML table. The formatting for the table is a little more elaborate and will require defining the table, and cell headers. You will notice the use of standard SharePoint CSS classes being referenced.

```
case displayMode.Table:
  boolbAltRow = true;
  messages.AppendFormat(@"<table width='100%' border='0'
  cellpadding='1' cellspacing='0' class='ms-listviewtable'>
  <tr class='ms-viewheadertrms-vhltr'>");
  messages.AppendFormat(@"<td>Title</td><td>Workflow</td>
  <td>Status</td><td>Start Date</td><td>Due Date</td></tr>");
```

20. We will then add in a `foreach` loop to iterate through the rows within the results `DataTable` object. For each row we will format the results within the table cells and use the `bAltRow` Boolean value to control whether to use the alternating styles class `ms-alternatingstrong`. Afterwards we terminate the loop, close out the `table` and `div` tags, `break` the `case` block, and terminate the `switch` block.

```
foreach (DataRow row in results.Rows)
{
  messages.AppendFormat(@"<tr ");
  if (bAltRow) { messages.AppendFormat(@"class=
  'ms-alternatingstrong'"); }
  messages.AppendFormat(@"><td>
  <a href=""javascript:showTask('{0}', '{1}',
  '{2}')"">{1}</a></td><td>{2}</td><td>{3}</td><td></td>

  <td></td></tr>", row[1].ToString(), row[0].ToString(),
  row[4].ToString(), row[3].ToString());
  bAltRow = !bAltRow;
}
messages.AppendFormat(@"</table></div>");
break;
```

21. With the output string fully generated we will ensure that the controls
    have been initialized, and set the output Literal control to the messages
    StringBuilder object and close the try block. We then have a catch block
    that can trap any exceptions that might have occurred, and use the output
    Literal control to display the exception details.

```
  this.EnsureChildControls();
  this._output.Text = messages.ToString();
}
catch (Exception ex)
{
  this.EnsureChildControls();
  this._output.Text+= "Error: " + ex.Message.ToString();
}
```

Creating the MyTasks.js file

The MyTasks.js script referenced within the Display() function is used to leverage
the Client OM's modal dialog framework for displaying the tasks within a standard
modal window.

When using JavaScript within your custom Web Parts, it is often easiest to add the
content to a file that is managed with the custom Web Part's feature. By mapping
the Layouts folder in your Visual Studio project, it is possible to deploy files to a
location within the Layouts virtual directory making it available to any site in
the farm.

Best practice is to name the folder to match your project or feature name. In this case
a folder named SPBlueprints.MyTasks has been added and the following MyTasks.
js script was added to the project:

```
function showTask(taskLink, title, workflow) {
  var _options = { url: taskLink, width: '800', title: workflow +
  ' - ' +   title };
  SP.UI.ModalDialog.showModalDialog(_options);
}
```

MyTasks Web Part

The MyTasks Web Part will utilize the SiteData approach to pull together a listing
of all the user's tasks by executing the GetSiteData() method from a specified list
of sites.

Creating the Web Part

The MyTasks Web Part will be added to the `SPBlueprints.MyTasks` project.

To create the solution and Web Part:

1. Open the `SPBlueprints.MyTasks` project in Visual Studio 2010.
2. Browse the Installed Templates and select **Visual C# | SharePoint 2010**.
3. Right click on the project file and select **Add | New Item**.
4. From the template selection screen select the **Web Part** option.
5. Provide the **Name** as `MyTasks` and click on the **Add** button as shown in the following screenshot:

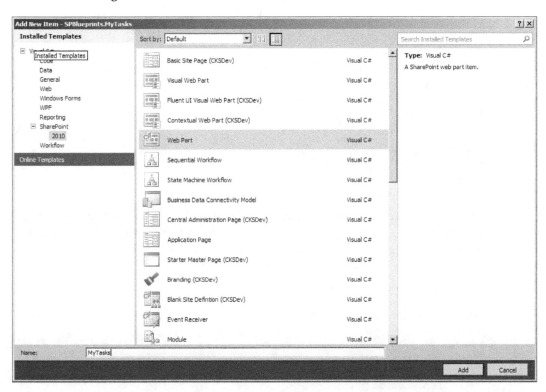

6. Edit the `MyTasks.webpart` file and add in the custom properties shown as follows:

```
<property name="Title" type="string">MyTasks</property>
<property name="Description" type="string">Task Rollup Web
  Part</property>
<property name="DisplayMode" type="string">List</property>
```

7. The following namespaces need to be added to the default namespaces listed with a new Web Part template:

```
using System.Data;
using System.Text;
```

8. The Web Part will include a number of properties that help to manage both the processing and the output of the content. First we will define the Display Mode property, which is used to determine the format of the output using a simple enumeration to designate a List or Table format.

```
private displayMode _displayMode;
public enum displayMode
{
  List,
  Table
}

[WebBrowsable(true),
  Category("Configuration"),
  WebDisplayName("Display Mode"),
  WebDescription("Please select the display mode."),
  Personalizable(PersonalizationScope.Shared)]
public displayMode DisplayMode
{
  get { return _displayMode; }
  set { _displayMode = value; }
}
```

9. The next property will be another enumeration that will determine whether to aggregate tasks from just the current site collection or to use the specified list of sites.

```
private scope _scope;
public enum scope
{
  Current,
  Specified
}
[WebBrowsable(true),
  Category("Configuration"),
  WebDisplayName("Scope"),
  WebDescription("Please select the scope to search for
    tasks."),
  Personalizable(PersonalizationScope.Shared)]
public scope Scope
{
  get { return _scope; }
  set { _scope = value; }
}
```

10. Last we will specify the site list which is a comma-delimited list of sites the site designer can specify for inclusion in the rollup.

```
private string _siteList;

[WebBrowsable(true),
  Category("Configuration"),
  WebDisplayName("Site List"),
  WebDescription("Please provide a comma delimited list of
    sites"),
  Personalizable(PersonalizationScope.Shared)]
public string SiteList
{
  get { return _siteList; }
  set { _siteList = value; }
}
```

11. The output will be built within a `Literal` control defined within the class, and instantiated within the `CreateChildControls()` method shown as follows:

```
protected Literal _output;
protected override void CreateChildControls()
{
  this._output = newLiteral();
  this._output.ID = "output";
  this.Controls.Add(this._output);
}
```

12. The `LoadTasks()` method will load the task information for both display modes. It will take in the site list parameter and return a `DataTable` object. To start off the method we will prepare some variables and objects used within this block of code. The `DataTable` object results will be used to store the master list of results, while the `DataTable` object `localResults` will contain temporary results from one specified site collection. We will also get the current user's display name which will be used within the query.

```
private DataTable LoadTasks(string siteList)
{
DataTable results = new DataTable();
DataTable localResults = new DataTable();
bool firstRow = true;
SPWeb web = null;
string[] siteArray = siteList.Split(',');
string user =

  SPContext.Current.Web.CurrentUser.Name.ToString();
```

13. Next we will create and set the `SPSiteDataQuery` object which will be used to define the query. As discussed previously, the `Lists` property can be used to filter the results for a specific template type, in this case the Tasks template, which has an internal ID of 107.

```
SPSiteDataQuery query = newSPSiteDataQuery();
query.Lists = "<Lists ServerTemplate=\"107\" />";
```

14. The `ViewFields` property will contain the CAML query that specifies the fields you want to retrieve. For any fields that will not return a matching value, be sure to set the `Nullable = True` property to ensure that it is returned.

```
query.ViewFields = "<FieldRef Name=\"LinkTitle\" />"+
  "<FieldRef Name=\"Title\" />" +
  "<FieldRef Name=\"AssignedTo\" Nullable=\"TRUE\"/>"+
  "<FieldRef Name=\"StartDate\" Nullable=\"TRUE\"/>" +
  "<FieldRef Name=\"DueDate\" Nullable=\"TRUE\"/>" +
  "<FieldRef Name=\"Status\" Nullable=\"TRUE\"/>" +
  "<FieldRef Name=\"PercentComplete\" Nullable=\"TRUE\"/>" +
  "<FieldRef Name=\"WorkflowName\" Nullable=\"TRUE\"/>" +
  "<ListProperty Name=\"Title\" />" +
  "<FieldRef Name=\"ID\" />" +
  "<FieldRef Name=\"EncodedAbsUrl\" />" +
  "<FieldRef Name=\"FileDirRef\" />";
```

15. Next is the `Query` property, which will specify the `Where` and `OrderBy` clauses. For this example, we want to find tasks that are assigned to the current user with a status not equal to completed, and then order the results by the `StartDate` field.

```
query.Query = "<Where><And><Eq><FieldRef Name=\"AssignedTo\"
/>" +
"<Value Type=\"User\">" + user + "</Value></Eq>" +
"<Neq><FieldRef Name=\"Status\" />" +
"<Value Type=\"Choice\">Completed</Value></Neq></And></Where>"
+
"<OrderBy><FieldRef Name=\"StartDate\" /></OrderBy>";
```

16. The last two properties we will set are the `Webs` property which will set it to look at the entire site collection, and then we will set the `RowLimit` property.

```
query.Webs = "<Webs Scope=\"SiteCollection\" />";
query.RowLimit = 100;
```

17. As the Web Part supports two different processing models, we will use the `Scope` Web Part property within a `switch` statement to determine which block to execute. Please note that `Current` scope is the default scope.

18. For the `Specified` scope, we will iterate through `siteArray` and connect to the `SPSite` object for each specified item. For each site, we will set a reference to its `RootWeb`, and then execute the `GetSiteData()` method passing in the `SPSiteDataQuery` object, and populating the results in the `localResults` `DataTable` object.

```
switch (_scope)
{
  case scope.Specified:
    for (int i = 0; i <= siteArray.GetUpperBound(0); i++)
      {
        using (SPSite site = new SPSite(siteArray[i]))
        {
          web = site.RootWeb;
          localResults = web.GetSiteData(query);
```

19. If this is the first time through we will need to set the `results` `DataTable` equal to the `localResults` `DataTable` which will also pass in the schema information, otherwise we will execute the `Merge()` method of `DataTable` which will add the rows from the `localResults` `DataTable` into the results `DataTable`. We then set the `firstRow` value to `false` so that the next load will be merged.

```
if (firstRow)
  results = localResults;
else
  results.Merge(localResults);

firstRow = false;
```

20. Next, we need to close out the `switch` block and add the `break` command to ensure that future blocks are not executed.

```
    }
}
break;
```

21. The `default` block of the `switch` statement is used to process results only for the current site. As we are not aggregating results at this point, the overall code is significantly simpler. We will get a reference to the current web and populate the `results` `DataTable` directly.

```
default:  //Current Site
  web = SPContext.Current.Web;
  results = web.GetSiteData(query);
  break;
}
```

22. At the very end we will set the method's return to the `results DataTable` to ensure that the data is passed back to the calling method.

```
return results;
```

23. The `FormatLink()` method will be used within the `Display()` method to provide standard formatting to the task links within each of the display modes. The `FileDirRef` field needs to be manipulated in order to get the path to the item. We will read out the value to a local variable and then execute a `split` command on it using the `'#'` character, which is included in the multipart value. Finally we will format the `return` value with a full link to the item, including the `QueryString` command, so that it assumes the modal dialog styles and includes the proper source value.

```
private string FormatLink(string FileRef, string AbsUrl,
  string itemID)
{
    string[] listPath = FileRef.Split('#');
    return AbsUrl + listPath[1] + "/DispForm.aspx?ID="
    + itemID + "&IsDlg=1&Source="
    + HttpContext.Current.Request.Url.ToString();
}
```

24. With all of the setup work complete, we can now define the `Display()` method that can be called from the `OnLoad()` method. The method starts by defining the `StringBuilder` object we will use to build the output of the Web Part, and then calls the `LoadTasks()` method we just defined to load the actual data.

```
protected void Display()
{
    StringBuilder messages = new StringBuilder();
try
{
    DataTable results = LoadTasks(_siteList);
```

25. Next we will start to format the output with the `MyTasks` label, specify the number of results that were returned, specify the selected scope and create a `div` container to hold our content.

```
messages.AppendFormat(@"<br>My Tasks: {0} ({1})",
  results.Rows.Count, _scope);
messages.AppendFormat(@"<div id='MyTasks'><ul>");
```

26. Then we will reference the `MyTasks.js` file specified in the next section which will be used to load our task items within a standard model dialog. This gives the user access to the standard task or workflow task forms on the specified site, without having to click away from the page they are on.

```
messages.AppendFormat(@"<script type='text/ecmascript'
 src='/_layouts/SPBlueprints.MyTasks/MyTasks.js'></script>");
```

27. To handle the multiple display modes, we will use another `switch` statement that keys off the Display Mode field. The first block will handle the list display mode in which we will create a loop to iterate the rows in the results `DataTable` object.

```
switch (_displayMode)
{
  case displayMode.List:
    foreach (DataRow row in results.Rows)
    {
```

28. Within the loop we will define and populate a number of row-level variables used in the processing of the row output. To get the task item's formatted link we will call the `FormatLink()` method passing in the `FileDirRef`, `EncodedAbsURL,` and `ID` fields for the row. We will also apply some conditional formatting for the `WorkflowName` row, showing the value in brackets if it is returned, or ignoring it if it is not.

```
itemLink = FormatLink(row["FileDirRef"].ToString(),
 row["EncodedAbsUrl"].ToString(), row["ID"].ToString());
string workflow = "";
if (row["WorkflowName"].ToString() != "")
  workflow = "(" + row["WorkflowName"].ToString() + ")";
```

29. With the link value formatted we can now write it to the output including the call to the `showTask()` method within the `MyTasks.js` file referenced earlier.

```
messages.AppendFormat(@"<li>
 <a href=""javascript:showTask('{2}', '{0}', '{1}')"">{0}</a>
 {1}</li>", row["Title"].ToString(), workflow, itemLink);
```

30. We can now complete our `foreach` block, close our `list` and `div` HTML objects and add the `break` command within the `case` block.

```
}
messages.AppendFormat(@"</ul></div>");
break;
```

31. The second `case` within the `switch` block is used for the table display mode, which will format a grid-like output through the use of a simple HTML table.

```
case displayMode.Table:
  bool bAltRow = true;
  messages.AppendFormat(@"<table width='100%' border='0'
   cellpadding='1' cellspacing='0' class='ms-listviewtable'>
   <tr class='ms-viewheadertrms-vhltr'>");
  messages.AppendFormat(@"<td>Title</td><td>Workflow</td>
   <td>Status</td><td>% Complete</td><td>Start Date</td><td>
   Due Date</td></tr>");
```

32. To process the results we use a `foreach` loop to iterate through the data rows within the results `DataTable`. Similar to the list display mode we will make a call to the `FormatLink()` method passing in the `FileDirRef`, `EncodedAbsURL`, and `ID` fields for the row.

```
foreach (DataRow row in results.Rows)
{
  itemLink = FormatLink(row["FileDirRef"].ToString(),
  row["EncodedAbsUrl"].ToString(), row["ID"].ToString());
```

33. We can now format the table row which includes support for the `ms-alternatingstrong` style through the use of a simple Boolean variable that checks if the value was changed with each row. The main table cell values are also written out with the main value formatted as a link to the `showTask()` method from the `MyTasks.js` file.

```
messages.AppendFormat(@"<tr ");
if (bAltRow) { messages.AppendFormat(@"class='ms-
 alternatingstrong'"); }
messages.AppendFormat(@"><td>
 <a href=""javascript:showTask('{0}', '{1}',
 '{2}')"">{1}</a></td><td>{2}</td><td>{3}</td><td>{4}</td>
 <td>{5}</td><td>{6}</td></tr>", itemLink,
 row["Title"].ToString(), row["WorkflowName"].ToString(),
 row["Status"].ToString(), row["PercentComplete"],
 row["StartDate"], row["DueDate"]);
bAltRow = !bAltRow;
```

34. We can now terminate the loop block, close our `table` container, complete our `switch` block, and close our `div` container.

```
  }
  messages.AppendFormat(@"</table>");
  break;
}
messages.AppendFormat(@"</div>");
```

35. With all of the formatting within the `Display()` method complete we will now make a call to the `EnsureChildControls()` method to make sure that everything is initialized, and then set the output `Literal` control to our messages variable before closing out the `try` block. A standard `catch` block has also been added to support exception handling.

```
    this.EnsureChildControls();
    this._output.Text = messages.ToString();
}
catch (Exception ex)
{
    this.EnsureChildControls();
    this._output.Text = "Error: " + ex.Message.ToString();
}
```

Displaying the MyTasks and MyTasks Search Web Parts

The display of the MyTasks and MyTasks Search Web Parts are identical and both support multiple display modes, a bulleted list as well as a table view.

The following is a screenshot of the MyTasks Web Part in a simple list mode:

The following is a screenshot of the MyTasks Web Part in table mode:

Both the list and table modes offer links directly to the tasks in a model window shown as follows:

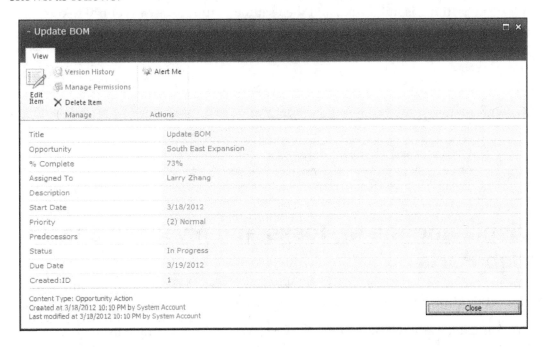

While the **All Items** link directs to the standard list item display form, workflow tasks will automatically redirect to the workflow task in the model form shown as follows:

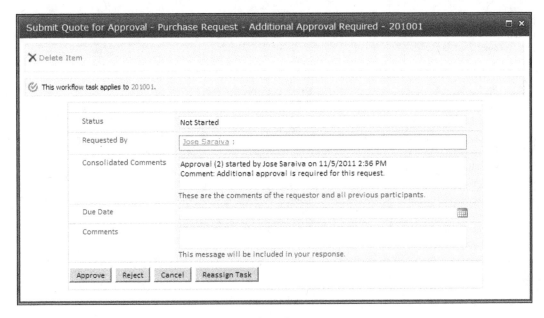

Completed SPBlueprints.MyTasks solution

The completed solution for the SPBlueprints.MyTasks project and Web Part feature should include both the MyTasks and MyTasksSearch Web Parts, and the MyTasks.js script file. The final **Solution Explorer** should look like the following screenshot:

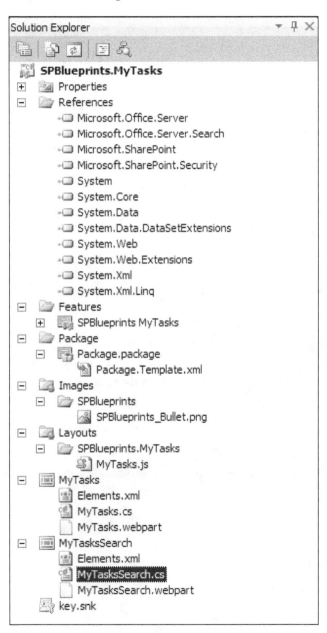

The completed feature definition should look like the following screenshot:

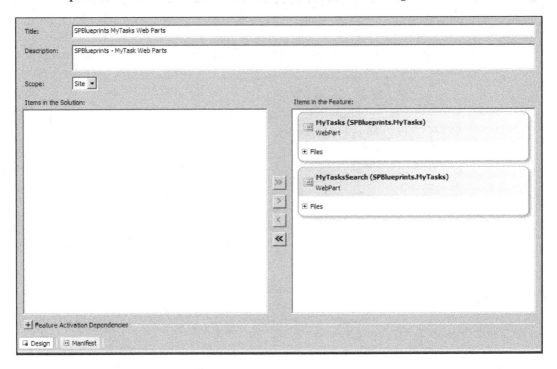

Summary

This chapter leveraged both the search index as well as the `SiteData` method for aggregating user tasks into a simple Web Part that can be displayed on main pages or on the user's My Content site.

We showed you how to create custom Web Parts that can aggregate tasks from the specified sites.

In the next chapter, we can take a look at how to create a site directory feature using SharePoint Search.

Building a Site Directory with SharePoint Search

9

A common challenge for many SharePoint users is finding sites with content that is relevant to them. It is pretty common to find environments with hundreds if not thousands of sites. In past versions of the product, there was a Site Directory feature that was available, but it was essentially just a SharePoint list which required manual entry and significant maintenance, which ultimately made it a pretty unreliable and ineffective solution.

This chapter will provide some alternative solutions for addressing these challenges, starting with an overview of some key concepts on how to leverage SharePoint Search to provide an optimized experience, making it easier for users to search and discover relevant sites. In addition to the conceptual overview, the following configurations and custom solutions will be covered:

- Sites Search Scope
- Site Directory page
- Relevant sites Web Part

Site Directory options

There are two main approaches to providing a Site Directory feature:

- A central list that has to be maintained
- Using a search-based tool that can provide the information dynamically

List-based Site Directory

With a list-based Site Directory, a list is provisioned in a central site collection, such as the root of a portal or intranet. Like all lists, site columns can be defined to help describe the site's metadata. Since it is stored in a central list, the information can easily be queried, which can make it easy to show a listing of all sites and perform filtering, sorting, and grouping, like all SharePoint lists.

It is important to consider the overall site topology within the farm. If everything of relevance is stored within a single site collection, a list-based Site Directory, accessible throughout that site collection, may be easy to implement. But as soon as you have a large number of site collections or web applications, you will no longer be able to easily use that Site Directory without creating custom solutions that can access the central content and display it on those other sites. In addition, you will need to ensure that all users have access to read from that central site and list.

Another downside to this approach is that the list-based Site Directory has to be maintained to be effective, and in many cases it is very difficult to keep up with this. It is possible to add new sites to the directory programmatically, using an event receiver, or as part of a process that automates the site creation, such as the solution outlined in *Chapter 5, Building a Site Request and Provisioning System*. However, through the site's life cycle, changes will inevitably have to be made, and in many cases sites will be retired, archived, or deleted.

While this approach tends to work well in small, centrally controlled environments, it does not work well at all in most of the large, distributed environments where the number of sites is expected to be larger and the rate of change is typically more frequent.

Search-based site discovery

An alternative to the list-based Site Directory is a completely dynamic site discovery based on the search system. In this case the content is completely dynamic and requires no specific maintenance. As sites are created, updated, or removed, the changes will be updated in the index as the scheduled crawls complete. For environments with a large number of sites, with a high frequency of new sites being created, this is the preferred approach.

The content can also be accessed throughout the environment without having to worry about site collection boundaries, and can also be leveraged using out of the box features, as we will see later in this chapter.

The downside to this approach is that there will be a limit to the metadata you can associate with the site. Standard metadata that will be related to the site include the site's name, description, URL, and to a lesser extent, the managed path used to configure the site collection. From these items you can infer keyword relevance, but there is no support for extended properties that can help correlate the site with categories, divisions, or other specific attributes.

How to leverage search

Most users are familiar with how to use the Search features to find content, but are not familiar with some of the capabilities that can help them pinpoint specific content or specific types of content. This section will provide an overview on how to leverage search to provide features that help support users finding results that are only related to sites.

Content classes

SharePoint Search includes an object classification system that can be used to identify specific types of items as shown in the next table. It is stored in the index as a property of the item, making it available for all queries.

Content Class	Description
STS_Site	Site Collection objects
STS_Web	Subsite/Web objects
STS_list_[templatename]	List objects where [templatename] is the name of the template such as Announcements or DocumentLibrary
STS_listitem_[templatename]	List Item objects where [templatename] is the name of the template such as Announcements or DocumentLibrary
SPSPeople	User Profile objects (requires a User Profile Service Application)

The **contentclass** property can be included as part of an ad hoc search performed by a user, included in the search query within a customization, or as we will see in the next section, used to provide a filter to a Search Scope.

Search Scopes

Search Scopes provide a way to filter down the entire search index. As the index grows and is filled with potentially similar information, it can be helpful to define Search Scopes to put specific set of rules in place to reduce the initial index that the search query is executed against. This allows you to execute a search within a specific context. The rules can be set based on the specific location, specific property values, or the crawl source of the content.

The Search Scopes can be either defined centrally within the Search service application by an administrator or within a given Site Collection by a Site Collection administrator. If the scope is going to be used in multiple Site Collections, it should be defined in the Search service application. Once defined, it is available in the Search Scopes dropdown box for any ad hoc queries, within the custom code, or within the Search Web Parts.

Defining the Site Directory Search Scope

To support dynamic discovery of the sites, we will configure a Search Scope that will look at just site collections and subsites. As we saw above, this will enable us to separate out the site objects from the rest of the content in the search index. This Search Scope will serve as the foundation for all of the solutions in this chapter.

To create a custom Search Scope:

1. Navigate to the **Search Service Application**.
2. Click on the **Search Scopes** link on the **QuickLaunch** menu under the **Queries** and **Results** heading.
3. Set the **Title** field to **Site Directory**.
4. Provide a **Description**.

5. Click on the **OK** button as shown in the following screenshot:

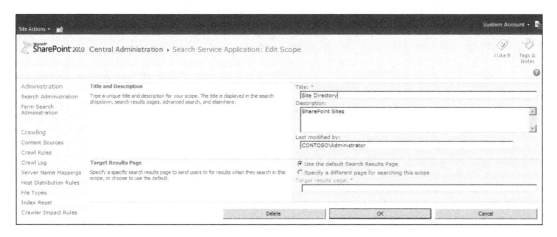

6. From the **View Scopes** page, click on the **Add Rules** link next to the new Search Scope.

7. For the **Scope Rule Type** select the **Property Query** option.

8. For the **Property Query** select the **contentclass** option.

9. Set the property value to **STS_Site**.

10. For the **Behavior** section, select the **Include** option.

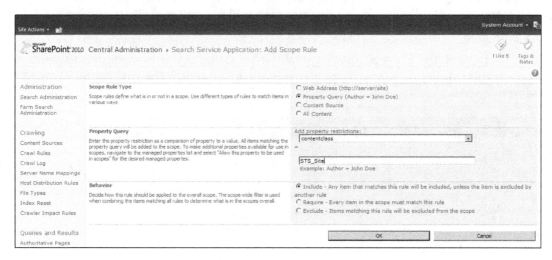

11. From the **Scope Properties** page, select the **New Rule** link.

12. For the **Scope Rule Type** section, select the **Property Query** option.

13. For the **Property Query** select the **contentclass** option.

14. Set the property value to **STS_Web**.

15. For the **Behavior** section, select the **Include** option.

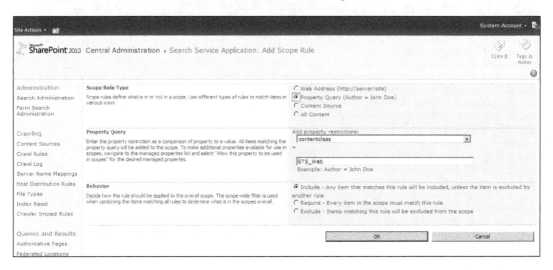

The end result will be a Search Scope that will include all Site Collection and subsite entries. There will be no user generated content included in the search results of this scope.

After finishing the configuration for the rules there will be a short delay before the scope is available for use. A scheduled job will need to compile the search scope changes.

Once compiled, the **View Scopes** page will list out the currently configured search scopes, their status, and how many items in the index match the rules within the search scopes.

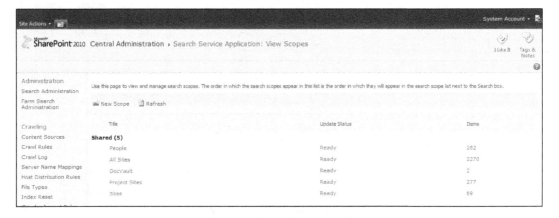

4. Select the **View All Pages** action.

5. Select the **Documents** tab.

6. Click the **New Document** action and select **Page** as shown in the next screenshot:

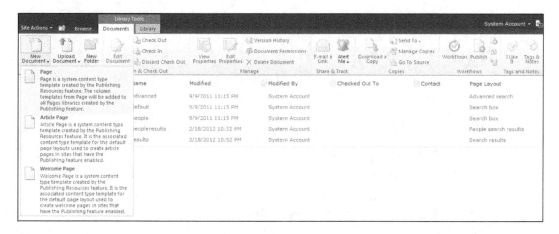

7. Set the **Title** field to the value **Site Directory**.

8. Provide a **Description**.

9. Provide a **URL Name** such as **Site-Directory**.

10. Ensure that for the **Page Layout, (Welcome Page) Search results** is selected.

11. Click on the **Create** button.

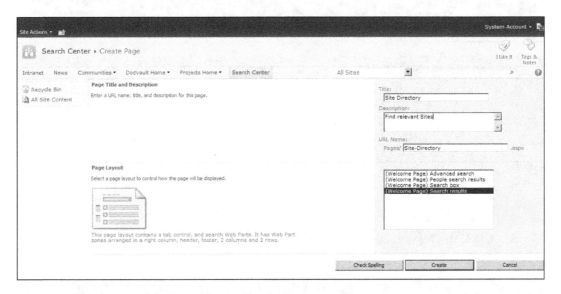

Configure the Site Directory page settings

We will now see a standard search results page and will need to make a few minor changes in order to be used to support the Site Directory requirements.

To configure the page's settings:

1. Click on **Site Actions | Edit Page**.

2. From **Search Box Web Part**, select the **Edit Web Part** action.

3. Within the **Miscellaneous** section, change the **Target search results page URL** to **Site-Directory.aspx** so that it directs the request to our Site Directory page.

4. Click the **OK** button.

5. From the **Search Core Results** Web Part, select the **Edit Web Part** action.

6. Within the **Location Properties** section, set the **Scope property** to **Site Directory**.

7. Within the **More Results Link Options**, check the checkbox to **Show More Results Link**.

8. Click on the **OK** button.

Adding a Site Directory tab

With both the search query and result pages there is a control that will display contextual tabs that can be used to navigate to customized search pages. The **All Sites** and **People** tabs are added by default, but additional tabs can be configured. To make it easy for users to search the Site Directory from the Search Center, we will add a Site Directory tab. Please note, since the values are stored in a set of central lists within the Search Center, you only need to configure the tabs once for the regular search pages and once for the results pages.

To add a new tab:

1. Click on the **Add New Tab** option under the existing tabs.
2. Set the **Tab Name** property to **Site Directory**.
3. Set the **Page** property to **Site-Directory.aspx**.
4. Set the **Tooltip** property to **Click** for relevant sites.
5. Click on the **Save** button.

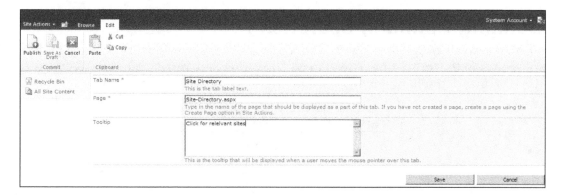

Common Searches

The search system's query engine is extremely powerful, but most users are not familiar enough with how to format the queries for advanced searches. A great way to address this is by providing a list of common search keywords and saved queries. This will allow users to quickly and easily initiate a search and it will work with the Refinement Web Part to provide additional drill through capabilities.

This Common Searches information can be saved in a simple link list within the Search Center. Like the search tabs feature, this provides an easy way for the Search Center administrator to maintain the configuration through the standard SharePoint UI. The standard link list template is sufficient, but if you want to potentially have different lists for different search tabs, then I recommend that you add a lookup field to the Tab Name field of the Tabs in Search Results list. A sample view of the list is displayed in the next screenshot:

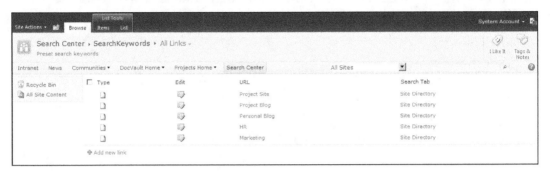

Defining Common Searches

Adding a saved search is as simple as adding an entry to the link list. The key to this solution is in the formatting of the linked URL. There are three main parameters in the URL that you will frequently need to use.

Parameter	Description
k	Keyword
s	Search Scope
r	Refiner

Here are some examples used to power up the demo in the book.

Simple saved query

In its simplest form, keywords are passed to the results page in the URL's query string. This is the same result as a user passing in a simple keyword in the search box. It might look like this: `http://intranet/search2/Pages/Site-Directory.aspx?k=HR`.

The URL can be separated into two parts with the first part being the path to the results page: `http://intranet/search2/Pages/Site-Directory.aspx`, and the remaining part which identifies the keyword query that will be executed: `k=HR`.

Advanced saved query

Through the query language it is possible to specify additional keywords and logical operations. The following example will search for Blog subsites and apply a refiner to ensure that any returned sites are within the MySites area.

The query would look like this: `k=Blog&r=site%3D%22http%3A%2F%2Fintranet%2F my%2Fpersonal%22`.

The keyword part is set to `k=Blog`. The refiner part is set to `r=site%3D%22http%3A%2 F%2Fintranet%2Fmy%2Fpersonal%22`.

Adding Common Searches to the Site Directory page

To add the **Common Searches** list to the Site Directory page we will simply add a standard list view set to the summary view, which will present a bulleted list. Additional properties can be set to change the title and overall display if desired. Alternatively this can be displayed via a Client OM script or a Server OM Web Part if additional control is needed over the rendered display.

Site Directory displayed

The completed Site Directory page with the Common Searches listing is displayed in the following screenshot:

A close up view of the **Common Searches** list view Web Part is displayed in the following screenshot:

Related sites Web Part

In addition to making it easy for the users to execute ad hoc site searches, it may also be valuable to dynamically display a listing of related web sites. To provide this feature, one approach would be to create a Web Part that allows the site owner to specify some related keywords, and then perform the Site Directory search and display a list of relevant sites.

Creating the Web Part

The Related sites Web Part will be added to the previously created SPBlueprints. WebParts project created in *Chapter 2, Building an Out of Office Delegation Solution*.

To add the additional Web Part:

1. Open the SPBlueprints.WebParts project in Visual Studio 2010.
2. Browse the installed templates and select **Visual C# | SharePoint 2010**.
3. Right-click on the project file and select **Add | New Item**.
4. From the template selection screen select the **Web Part** option.
5. Provide the name **RelatedSites** and click on the **Add** button.
6. Edit the RelatedSites.webpart file, and add in the custom properties as shown in the following:

   ```
   <property name="Title" type="string">Related Sites</property>
   <property name="Description" type="string">SPBlueprints - The
   Related Sites web part will search for sites with matching
   keywords.</property>
   <property name="SearchProxyName" type="string">Search Service
   Application</property>
   ```

```
<property name="SearchScopeName" type="string">Site Directory</
property>
<property name="DisplayLimit" type="int">5</property>
<property name="KeywordList" type="string">sites</property>
```

7. Start by editing the `RelatedSites.cs` file and add in the following references:

```
using System.Collections;
using System.Data;
using System.Text;
using Microsoft.SharePoint.Administration;
using Microsoft.Office.Server.Search;
using Microsoft.Office.Server.Search.Query;
using Microsoft.Office.Server.Search.Administration;
```

8. Next we will need to define the Web Part's properties starting with the Search Proxy Name property. This property will be used to manage the connection to the Search service application.

```
private string _searchProxyName;

[WebBrowsable(true),
 Category("Configuration"),
 WebDisplayName("Search Proxy Name"),
 WebDescription("Please provide the name of your Search Service
Application."),
 Personalizable(PersonalizationScope.Shared)]
public string SearchProxyName
{
  get { return _searchProxyName; }
  set { _searchProxyName = value; }
}
```

9. Next we will define the Search Scope Name property which can be used to target the desirable content for display.

```
private string _searchScopeName;
[WebBrowsable(true),
 Category("Configuration"),
 WebDisplayName("Search Scope Name"),
 WebDescription("Please provide the name of your Search Scope."),
 Personalizable(PersonalizationScope.Shared)]
public string SearchScopeName
{
  get { return _searchScopeName; }
  set { _searchScopeName = value; }
}
```

10. Next we will define the Display Limit property used to determine how many records to display.

```
private int _displayLimit;
[WebBrowsable(true),
 Category("Configuration "),
 WebDisplayName("Result limit"),
 WebDescription("The number of items to display."),
 Personalizable(PersonalizationScope.Shared)]
public int DisplayLimit
{
  get { return _displayLimit; }
  set { _displayLimit = value; }
}
```

11. Next we will define the Keywords property where the site administrator will actually set the keywords.

```
private string _keywordList;
[WebBrowsable(true),
 Category("Configuration"),
 WebDisplayName("Keywords"),
 WebDescription("Comma delimited list of keywords"),
 Personalizable(PersonalizationScope.Shared)]
public string KeywordList
{
  get { return _keywordList; }
  set { _keywordList = value; }
}
```

12. The output will be built within a Literal control defined within the class, and instantiated within the CreateChildControls() method as shown in the following:

```
protected Literal _output;
protected override void CreateChildControls()
{
  this._output = new Literal();
  this._output.ID = "output";
  this.Controls.Add(this._output);
}
```

13. With all of the setup work complete, we can now define the `Display()` method that can be called from the `OnLoad()` method. The method starts by defining `StringBuilder` that we will use to build the output of the Web Part, and then checks to see if there are any keywords set. Since the keywords are stored within a single string property and are comma delimited, we will do a simple split command to load the values into an array. If there are no keywords, there will be no content to display.

```
protected void Display()
{
   StringBuilder messages = new StringBuilder();
   string[] keywords = this._keywordList.Split(',');
   if (keywords[0] != "")
   {
```

14. Next we attempt to connect to the Search Proxy specified in the Web Part properties. There is a `try/catch` block here in order to handle issues related to connecting to the Search service application differently than errors returned as part of a search.

```
try
{
   SearchQueryAndSiteSettingsServiceProxy settingsProxy = SPFarm.
Local.ServiceProxies.GetValue<SearchQueryAndSiteSettingsServicePro
xy>();
   SearchServiceApplicationProxy searchProxy = settingsProxy.
ApplicationProxies.GetValue<SearchServiceApplicationProxy>(this.
searchProxyName);

// Query and Display of Web Part

Catch
{
   this.EnsureChildControls();
   this._output.Text = "Error: Please specify a Search Service
Application.";
}
```

15. Now we can instantiate `FullTestSqlQuery` and prepare the data objects.

```
FullTextSqlQuery mQuery = new FullTextSqlQuery(searchProxy);
try
{
  ResultTableCollection resultsTableCollection;
  DataTable results = new DataTable();
```

16. The formatted query will be broken into two parts, with the first part being the same in all cases and then the addition of the dynamic keywords with a variable number of items. We will then define a simple `for` loop to append the query to include a dynamic part that covers each keyword. Since we are looking for matches for any of the keywords, the OR operator will be used, which will require that we set the scope predicate starting with the second keyword. The query can also be tailored to exclude other content in your environment as needed.

```
mQuery.QueryText = "SELECT Title, Path, SiteName FROM SCOPE()
Where ";
for (int i = 0; i <= keywords.GetUpperBound(0); i++)
{
  if (i > 0) mQuery.QueryText += " OR ";
  mQuery.QueryText += " ((\"scope\" = '" + _searchScopeName + "')
AND Contains('" + keywords[i] + "'))";
}
```

17. The remaining `FullTextSqlQuery` properties can now be set and the query executed. The returned `DataTable` object can now be checked for results to see if the list needs to be rendered.

```
mQuery.ResultTypes = ResultType.RelevantResults;
mQuery.TrimDuplicates = true;
mQuery.RowLimit = DisplayLimit;

resultsTableCollection = mQuery.Execute();
if (resultsTableCollection.Count > 0)
{
  ResultTable relevantResults = resultsTableCollection[ResultType.
RelevantResults];
  results.Load(relevantResults, LoadOption.OverwriteChanges);
```

18. The output can be as simple or as complex as needed. For this example, I will create a simple HTML bulleted list with a link to the site. A DIV container and the list will be defined, and then we will iterate through the rows, and write out each link.

```
messages.AppendFormat(@"<div id='RelatedSites'><ul>");
foreach (DataRow row in results.Rows)
{
  messages.AppendFormat(@"<li><a href='{1}'>{0}</a></li>",
row["Title"].ToString(), row["Path"].ToString(), row["SiteName"].
ToString());
}
messages.AppendFormat(@"</ul></div>");
}
```

19. With the display complete we can now render the output, complete the catch block to handle any exceptions, and dispose our Query object.

```
this.EnsureChildControls();
this._output.Text = messages.ToString();
}
catch (Exception ex)
{
  this.EnsureChildControls();
  this._output.Text = "Error: " + ex.Message.ToString();
}
finally
{
 mQuery.Dispose();
}
```

Display Related sites Web Part

Once deployed, the Related sites Web Part can be configured to set the desired keywords in a comma delimited list. The rendered screen is shown as follows:

Summary

This chapter leveraged the search features and configuration along with the Server OM to create a set of solutions that can be used to provide users with easy and intuitive ways to locate relevant sites.

The customizations are grouped as follows:

- Visual Studio 2010
    - **Web Part**: Creating a custom Web Part that can display related sites based on a keyword property.
- Browser based configuration
    - **Configure Search Scopes**: Create a Search Scope that automatically filters the content to show only site objects, and excludes any other type of content.
    - **Search Results Page**: A custom search results page that works with our custom search scope, and also includes some additional Web Parts to enhance the user's ability to find relevant sites.
    - **Configure Core Results Web Part**: The Core Results Web Part was configured to show our Site Directory and interactive search results.

This chapter showed how you can develop effective solutions that provide easy ways for users to find the relevant sites and resources needed to ensure better collaboration and process efficiency. These solutions are very easy to implement and can deliver immediate value.

Index

Symbols

__Context property 60

A

accountname variable 76
Add button 31
Add() method 154
addStatus function 21
appropriate use and incident dialog
  approach 25
  building 25
  displaying 26, 27
  form, displaying 25, 26
AssignTo property 62

B

BaseConfigurationID property 167
BaseTemplateID property 167
BaseTemplateName property 167
blank site, intranet site template 7
Blank Web Part page layout 11
Browser-based configuration 43

C

centralized list, task rollup
  considerations 216
  using 216
CheckOutOfOfficeActivity.cs 60-66
CheckOutOfOfficeActivity
  elements.xml 66, 67
check out of office, sample workflow 68, 69
Check out of office workflow activity
  about 58

  approach 59
  OfOfficeActivity.cs 60-66
  OfOfficeActivity elements.xml 66, 67
  creating 59
  web.config authorizedType entry,
    adding 67
common searches, site directory page
  adding 249
  advanced save query 249
  defining 248
  simple saved query 248
communities user profile property
  creating 118, 119
communities
  mapping, as managed property 119
community landing page
  configuring 115-117
  creating 115, 117
community members
  about 117
  communities, mapping as managed
    property 119
  communities user profile property,
    creating 118, 119
community site
  collection features 114
  creating 113, 114
  member page, configuring 119
  member page, creating 120
  members search query,
    configuring 120, 121
  People Search Core Results Web Part,
    adding 120
  site features 115
  supporting features 114, 115

Thank you for buying
Microsoft SharePoint 2010 Business Application Blueprints

About Packt Publishing

Packt, pronounced 'packed', published its first book "Mastering phpMyAdmin for Effective MySQL Management" in April 2004 and subsequently continued to specialize in publishing highly focused books on specific technologies and solutions.

Our books and publications share the experiences of your fellow IT professionals in adapting and customizing today's systems, applications, and frameworks. Our solution based books give you the knowledge and power to customize the software and technologies you're using to get the job done. Packt books are more specific and less general than the IT books you have seen in the past. Our unique business model allows us to bring you more focused information, giving you more of what you need to know, and less of what you don't.

Packt is a modern, yet unique publishing company, which focuses on producing quality, cutting-edge books for communities of developers, administrators, and newbies alike. For more information, please visit our website: www.packtpub.com.

About Packt Enterprise

In 2010, Packt launched two new brands, Packt Enterprise and Packt Open Source, in order to continue its focus on specialization. This book is part of the Packt Enterprise brand, home to books published on enterprise software – software created by major vendors, including (but not limited to) IBM, Microsoft and Oracle, often for use in other corporations. Its titles will offer information relevant to a range of users of this software, including administrators, developers, architects, and end users.

Writing for Packt

We welcome all inquiries from people who are interested in authoring. Book proposals should be sent to author@packtpub.com. If your book idea is still at an early stage and you would like to discuss it first before writing a formal book proposal, contact us; one of our commissioning editors will get in touch with you.

We're not just looking for published authors; if you have strong technical skills but no writing experience, our experienced editors can help you develop a writing career, or simply get some additional reward for your expertise.

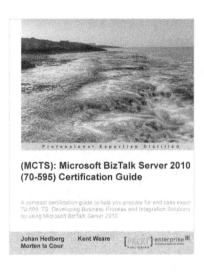

(MCTS): Microsoft BizTalk Server 2010
(70-595) Certification Guide

A compact certification guide to help you prepare and pass exam
70-595: TS: Developing Business Process and Integration Solutions
by using Microsoft BizTalk Server 2010

Johan Hedberg   Kent Weare
Morten la Cour

(MCTS): Microsoft BizTalk Server 2010 (70-595) Certification Guide

ISBN: 978-1-849684-92-7   Paperback: 476 pages

A compact certification guide to help you prepare for and pass exam 70-595: TS: Developing Business Process and Integration Solutions by using Microsoft BizTalk Server 2010

1. This book and e-book will provide all that you need to know in order to pass the (70-595) Developing Business Process and Integration Solutions exam by Using Microsoft BizTalk Server 2010 book

3. The layout and content of the book closely matches that of the skills measured by the exam, which makes it easy to focus your learning and maximize your study time in areas where you need improvement.

iPhone with Microsoft Exchange
Server 2010: Business Integration
and Deployment

Set up Microsoft Exchange Server 2010 and deploy iPhone and
other iDevices securely into your business

Steve Goodman

iPhone with Microsoft Exchange Server 2010: Business Integration and Deployment

ISBN: 978-1-849691-48-2   Paperback: 290 pages

Set up Microsoft Exchange Server 2010 and deploy iPhone and other iDevices securely into your business

1. Learn about Apple's mobile devices and how they work with Exchange Server 2010

2. Plan and deploy a highly available Exchange organization and Office 365 tenant

3. Create and enforce security policies and set up certificate-based authentication

Please check **www.PacktPub.com** for information on our titles

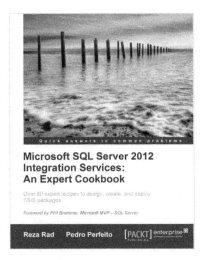

Microsoft SQL Server 2012
Integration Services:
An Expert Cookbook

ISBN: 978-1-849685-24-5   Paperback: 564 pages

Over 80 expert recipes to design, create, and deploy
SSIS packages

1. Full of illustrations, diagrams, and tips
    with clear step-by-step instructions and
    real time examples

2. Master all transformations in SSIS and their
    usages with real-world scenarios

3. Learn to make SSIS packages re-startable and
    robust; and work with transactions

4. Get hold of data cleansing and fuzzy operations
    in SSIS

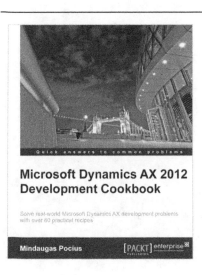

Microsoft Dynamics AX 2012
Development Cookbook

ISBN: 978-1-849684-64-4   Paperback: 372 pages

Solve real-world Microsoft Dynamics AX
development problems with over 80 practical recipes

1. Develop powerful, successful Dynamics AX
    projects with efficient X++ code with this book
    and eBook

2. Proven recipes that can be reused in numerous
    successful Dynamics AX projects

3. Covers general ledger, accounts payable,
    accounts receivable, project modules and
    general functionality of Dynamics AX

Please check **www.PacktPub.com** for information on our titles